The
Marketing
Edge

The Marketing Edge

A COLLECTION OF ARTICLES

PAUL FRANSON

WESTERN BOOK / JOURNAL PRESS
Printers & Publishers
SAN MATEO, CALIFORNIA

1989

ISBN: 0-936029-18-8
Library of Congress Catalog Number: 89-51639

Manufactured in the United States of America
By: Western Book / Journal Press
P.O. BOX 5226
San Mateo, California 94402
Library of Congress Cataloging-in-Publication Data:
    Franson, Paul
    The Marketing Edge

TABLE OF CONTENTS

INTRODUCTION

MARKETING

PUBLIC RELATIONS STRATEGIES

INTERNATIONAL

TACTICS 99

PUBLIC RELATIONS AGENCIES 171

Introduction

This book is a collection of slightly edited monthly columns written for *Adweek's Marketing Computers* and its predecessor, *Computer and Electronics Marketing,* from September 1984 to June 1989. A few articles were published elsewhere, are highly edited or original to this book.

The columns cover many subjects, ranging from basic marketing to public relations strategies and tactics.

I'd like to thank Judy Gonggryp, Mark Hamilton and Wendy Franson for their help in preparing the reprints for publication, and the editors of *Marketing Computers* for permission to use their copyrighted material.

Paul Franson

July 1989

MARKETING

Understand Technical Marketing

In the marketing of computers and electronics, two of the most distinct challenges are communicating with technical buyers and communicating with management.

Engineers are most interested in higher performance, new features, and being first. Managers want comfort. They must be convinced that their suppliers deliver quality products on time, will be in business a long time, and will give them their full support. That's why engineering magazines are continuously printing articles about hot new ideas and products from unknown but clever companies. Many of these firms don't survive and most miss promised product deadlines. Yet, engineers are excited about them.

The editors of some of these magazines rarely appear to weigh the credibility of the supplier carefully. Survey articles in these publications often give equal attention to products from a Hewlett-Packard or Motorola and to products from a two-person garage shop. That's not necessarily bad. After all, the garage where HP started still stands, and the same bright future may await some of these firms. But this situation helps explain seemingly capricious coverage in respected publications.

On the other hand, managers are most interested in information that discloses whether a prospective supplier will serve their real needs for delivery, reliability, and support. Most prefer to buy from large, well-known firms proven in their industries, though some believe that medium-sized vendors respond better than giants.

1

For this reason, publications read by managers — *Business Week, The Wall Street Journal, Electronic News,* and *Electronic Business,* for example — want to know about topics that answer questions about credibility. These publications are rarely interested in products unless they have significant impact on readers or markets. Most have little interest in small firms unless they are founded by well-known industry figures or involved in the month's hot topic, as most public relations people with start-up clients know well.

The business-oriented press is most interested in trends involving more than one company. They are also interested in a variety of other subjects, and this interest can help small firms who need to build credibility. Here are some of the subjects of most interest to this segment of the press:

Contracts. OEM deals, distribution, vendors, customers.

Financing. Private financing of large sums of money from well-known firms, initial and subsequent public offerings, corporate financing, large lines of credit.

Strategy. How companies intend to succeed in crowded marketplaces, or, perhaps even more difficult, how to succeed when they have to create a market.

Technology. Important new technologies, including licensing deals.

People. Additions, particularly if well-known, defections, and firings (unfortunately, one of the press' greatest interests).

Partnerships. Joint ventures, sales agreements.

Contrary to the belief of many people, communicating with engineers is fairly straightforward — even easy, if you follow the rules. They want details, specifications, and how-to material, not generalities. They're impressed with what's new, especially if it has new features and improved performance. The best channels for reaching engineers are product introductions, technical articles, technical news sections, hot news sections, staff-written surveys, and how-to application information.

Electronic engineering publications are successful partly because they know and serve their readers so well. This is a direct consequence of the engineering background of their staffs. Because of the engineering backgrounds of the editors, communicating with them on their terms is essential.

January 1985

Use Psychology In Marketing

As any computer or electronics marketer knows, many of the most interesting and powerful tools and techniques used to sell high-tech products originated in consumer marketing theory and practice.

One of the first consumer marketing techniques to influence sales of technical products was to make them more attractive and easy to use. An old-line instrument company didn't believe that engineers cared about looks or ease of use, just precision and accuracy. It's no longer in that business.

In the past, "positioning," the attempt to create a favorable hierarchical ranking in the minds of customers, has migrated from consumer to technical marketing jargon and practice.

During the last year, "event marketing" (staging happenings to get attention) has been the hot "new" technique. Next year, the marketing technique may be "psychomarketing" (to coin a phrase), which is understanding, analyzing, and exploiting the attitudes and motivations of consumers. Psychomarketing has seldom been applied to selling most technology-based products up to now, but it's a very popular technique in the consumer world.

Perhaps the best-known proponent of the technique is SRI International, the think tank that spun off from Stanford University Research Institute many years ago. SRI's Value and Lifestyle (VALS) program analyzes consumers, dividing them into nine categories based on their views of their place in society, self confidence, and buying patterns.

These and similar programs are designed to help marketers sell to consumers, not to business and industrial buyers. Yet, we can learn a lot from them. In the first place, many technical products are aimed at true consumers. Many personal computer marketing campaigns have been aimed squarely at home buyers — and have proved unsuccessful.

The fact is that even engineers and programmers are real people who share some of the same motivations that make some consumers buy $5,000 Piaget watches, others $10 Timexes.

Unfortunately, I am not yet aware of any rigorous study (if any social or psychological work can be so considered) that even attempts to understand the psychological patterns of corporate buyers. This appears to be fertile ground for some valuable work.

Nevertheless, we've learned through experience some lessons that have proved helpful in public relations.

The first problem with trying to exploit consumers' psyches via public relations, as opposed to advertising, is that we first have to understand the intermediary "customer," the press, analysts, and other influential third parties.

For example, there are some journalists who desire attention, recognition, and acceptance, yet are torn by conflicting impulses to remain independent. For that reason, a good relationship with the press often involves giving journalists attention, arranging personal and semi-social meetings with top executives, and making sure they know of your interest in them.

On the other hand, you can't treat a good reporter like an insider, a special friend of your company or your industry. That's not the reporter's job. You don't thank a reporter for writing a favorable story about your company or for helping your industry, but instead for doing a good job: digging, being accurate, adding insight and value.

Of course, different journalists have different attitudes. Anyone dealing with the press can try to take advantage of this situation. Many former journalists who now work in public relations are quite good at press contact because they understand the motivations involved. Other people adept at working with the press are often those who, in general, listen to and analyze the people they work with.

But it's hard to control the actual results that appear after talking to reporters. Public relations simply doesn't provide sufficient control, though doing an intensive and extensive (and shall we add, expensive?) job can help a great deal. But beyond the need to understand the press, analyzing the minds of customers is equally important

Let's look at some specifics. Buyers of hiqh-tech products fall into three categories: true consumers (buying for home or personal use), individuals buying for their own business use (individual professionals or managers), and group corporate or government purchases (typically involving more than one decision maker).

The existing research concentrates on consumers. Group purchases involve many conflicting forces, but security and comfort almost always play a major part. That's good news for IBM, HP, and Motorola, among others.

In some ways, individuals buying products that they will use themselves for some business purpose are most interesting. In this case, these people obviously share some of the motivations of traditional consumers. A Tektronix scope or HP voltmeter is a secure choice for an engineer, for example, while having a PC-based computer-aided-engineering or microprocessor development system obviously offers status.

Many engineers are quite conservative in personal taste and attitude, and are considered conventional. Conversely, others are innovators and want to be the first to own a product. They see status as a primary motivation.

There will be a great deal of discussion, adaptation, and application of psychomarketing in the years ahead. Let's just hope that its Orwellian overtones don't win out over fairness and ethics.

September 1985

Put Customers First

I'd like to direct this column to a marketing strategy whose time has come — concentrating on your customers.

The biggest topic of conversation among Silicon Valley inhabitants of late — believe it or not — isn't a computer, engineering or electronics company. It's Nordstrom.

For those of you who don't live in an area served by this upscale, Seattle-based department store chain, this comment, at a minimum, might seem somewhat bizarre. Though everyone knows we're supposed to be materialistic yuppies (not me, I'm too old), it's not the excellent styles and quality of the merchandise at Nordstrom that people are talking about. Instead, it's the service. At Nordstrom, the customer really does come first.

Whether in helpful, knowledgeable salespeople who go out of their way to serve you, or in their always-complete stock, or oneday alterations, or suits with two pairs of pants, or the delivery of merchandise and free gifts when they err, Nordstrom doesn't just claim to provide the best service. It does provide that service.

Interestingly, Nordstrom advertises little. Its competitors, like Macy's and Emporium-Capwell, spend heavily to reach consumers, who come to up-scale malls and visit their stores, yet end up buying from Nordstrom.

Not surprisingly, Macy's is responding aggressively, putting salespeople on commission and sending them to charm school in an effort to improve their performance.

I believe there is a strong message here for computer firms. Most keep looking for that elusive quality that will give them a strategic advantage over their competitors, but few seem to consider that putting the customer first may be the best way to accomplish this.

A few technology-based companies are known for strong support for their customers, both intermediate resellers and ultimate end-users, but they're rare. Two examples are Hewlett-Packard Co. and Software Publishing Corp.

For the last several years, HP's service and support has consistently ranked first in DataPro's annual independent survey of minicomputer and small business system users. Although most of the things that HP does to help customers are pretty obvious, many of HP's competitors just don't do them. For example, the company goes to extraordinary lengths to correct problems that sometimes inadvertently sneak into new products.

Software Publishing does something that seems unusual among computer and software companies. Though its current products are very sophisticated and powerful, they are easy to install and easy to use. And even though the firm's documentation is generally excellent, it's rarely needed because the products contain context-sensitive on-line help and intuitive operations. Users are rarely stumped.

That's thinking of your customers, a far contrast with the way that most software and computer products are sold to individuals today.

Most computer companies aren't very customer oriented and it's not hard to understand why. Traditionally, most sold primarily to sophisticated customers, notably engineers like themselves.

These customers needed little support, and they would often put up with poor documentation, delays and uneven quality. Some customers even took a perverse pride in correcting vendor problems as if they considered themselves very clever and smarter than the suppliers.

These traditional computer companies were internally oriented. Without determining whether there was any need for a product, they would conceive of, develop and build products, and then try to find customers who could use these products. Customers were almost an afterthought. You might call this self-directed marketing.

It's obvious that this attitude has to go, but I've seen little sign that most computer firms are doing more than paying lip service to customer support. Most have problems enough with large customers, and the system really bogs down for those small companies who buy in small quantities through dealers. Customers still resent paying for support and services even though most rationally know that dealers make low margins and have to charge for support.

But the typical customer correctly expects equipment to be easy to use and hard to break. To use another consumer analogy, most of us expect new cars to work, not break, and cost little to maintain. Only the most up-scale automobile suppliers like Mercedes and BMW have convinced their customers to expect to pay for expensive maintenance. Buyers of less-expensive products seem to have higher expectations for reliability without upkeep. The same is true with mainframes and personal computers. Mainframe buyers expect to spend more proportionally on maintenance and service than do buyers of inexpensive PC clones.

Inexpensive products that require extensive service will always be losers, but even upscale computer dealers seem to regard service as a nuisance and obstacle rather than a way to win friends and make money.

This self-directed marketing approach still serves for highly motivated buyers, particularly those leading-edge customers who always have to have the newest and highest performance in the products they buy. Nevertheless, I believe we'll be hearing more and more about the customer-oriented approach to marketing. The computer versions of companies like Nordstrom are going to have a big impact on our industry. I predict that we'll see some impressive successes from companies who adopt a customer orientation for selling computer products and services.

January 1988

Don't Forget the Forgotten Market
The Un-*Fortunate* 5 Million

Sometimes it seems as though almost every computer company in America is trying to sell exclusively to the Fortune 500 or 1,000 or 2,000. Sure, big corporations do buy a lot of computers, but a major reason this market is so attractive is that it is easy to address. Relatively few decision makers control vast purchases, simplifying the task for companies with direct sales forces. Even computer dealers such as Businessland and Entre are focusing on these big customers.

On top of that, customer support is easier when you sell to larger companies: Most are prepared to pay for it or do it themselves.

But what about the rest of American businesses? Who is selling computers to them?

Most of the five million small businesses in this country could improve their operations with the right computers, peripherals, software and services.

Almost 60 percent of the workers in the U.S. work in companies with fewer than 50 employees, yet those companies own few PCs. By contrast, less than 20 percent of the workforce is employed by Fortune 100-size companies (more than 1,000 employees) and most of these firms already own many PCs.

Obviously great opportunities exist for sales to smaller firms.

The biggest problems with selling to these small companies, however, are distribution channels, support requirements, and gaining visibility and credibility. Let's look at these problems and some possible solutions.

The first concern is distribution channels. At a glance, it seems simple: There are computer retailers in every city. In some cases, these are retailers who are extremely aggressive in selling computers at low prices. But these dealers tend to focus on selling to computer hobbyists and home users, not those whose livelihoods are dependent on computers. Ironically, they'll also attract large corporate suppliers, particularly those with strong internal support organizations. In fact, there have been situations where local dealers have underbid major computer makers on their own products.

These dealers aren't totally appropriate for the unsophisticated small business that needs a reliable computer to solve its problems today and tomorrow with little training necessary.

Most small businesses, in other words, want a turnkey solution. But they want to feel confident that someone will help them if they do experience any problems. It's like Sears' strategy for selling appliances: Their products may not always be the most exciting or the very best available, but they're good and most consumers believe that Sears services what it sells.

It's probably obvious that customer support is a huge problem for most computer dealers. Customers tend to want to buy computers at the lowest discount price they see advertised, then get support for free.

Perhaps the best supplier to small businesses is Tandy, whose Radio Shack stores sell computers in towns all over America. Tandy sells good, standardized products with solutions suitable for most small businesses and, like Sears, it services what it sells.

One of Tandy's big advantages is that it controls its pricing. It has excellent margins and doesn't face discounters across town selling the same product cheaper.

Another excellent way to reach small businesses is through specialists, notably those value-added resellers that serve geographic, vertical or horizontal slices of business. These firms typically offer customized products, insulating them somewhat from discount competition. The good ones have a sensitive and comprehensive customer orientation.

These specialists do particularly well with small companies in specific markets, since small companies like to buy from dedicated vendors with good reputations in their field.

Supporting small business can be difficult for the dealer. The vendor can help the dealer by producing reliable, easy-to-use products requiring little documentation yet providing excellent manuals and perhaps telephone hotline support.

Once you've solved the distribution and support problems, of course, you have to get visibility with small business. If a company is selling nationwide, almost any publication offers potential for public relations or even advertising, but it's a rare company that is able to afford or generate that interest. A few magazines specialize in small companies, such as *Inc.*, *Venture* and *CFO*, and they provide some opportunities, but there is basically no single publication appropriate to hit a wide range of owners of small businesses.

The situation is a bit simpler for specific markets, because virtually every business segment and function has specialized magazines and newspapers. Depending on the competition, it may be fairly easy to get attention from these organizations.

On the local level, opportunities are somewhat limited,

but there are local newspapers and magazines in virtually every community, and many are open to coverage of computer topics of interest to their readers. In particular, weekly newspapers, shoppers and local computer and business publications are great bets in smaller cities and towns, as are local broadcasters. It's tougher to get attention in larger cities, especially the most computer-literate such as Boston, Los Angeles, San Jose, and New York.

So it's definitely worth looking at selling to smaller businesses. The process entails problems and pitfalls, but the market is large — and it can be profitable for those firms that master it.

March 1987

Adapt Your Marketing Strategy
To High Technology

The art of marketing high-technology products to a business audience has evolved into a distinctive discipline, though its roots obviously lie partly in traditional consumer marketing, industrial marketing, and business-to-business marketing. None of these crafts, however, is adequate for the special problems we encounter in marketing computers and other technology-based products. The traditional education, experiences and references fail when tackling our particular circumstances.

Of course, not all technology products are sold in similar ways. The concerns noted by approval-oriented executives and selection-oriented engineers and managers differ significantly, and so do those of highly technical and less technical decision makers. Engineers, for example, are typically more interested in features and performance of products, while executives are concerned with the viability, staying power, and support of their prospective vendors.

This complicates the lives of most high-technology marketers, for we must usually address the concerns of both groups. In the consumer world, on the other hand, a common approach is to concentrate less on a vendor's reputation and more on the strong emotional reactions prompted by certain products and product lines.

An often overlooked reason for the complications of marketing high-technology products is that there is no common market for high technology. The markets are for specific types of products, and the customers have many concerns. Computers, for example, are bought by consumers for their children to play with. They are bought by home-business owners to manage their businesses. They're bought by small businesses as critical productivity tools, and by large organizations for purposes as diverse as reducing costs or making certain operations possible. Computers are bought as components of automation systems or as controllers for instruments or design systems. And finally, they are bought by resellers, systems integrators, distributors and dealers.

In short, marketing computers, or any high-technology product, means doing many different jobs, and it's evolved into a demanding special segment of the marketing world.

Let's look at how this situation has developed.

Most technology products are initially sold to sophisticated customers, who often use them to develop, design or manufacture other products. For this reason, the greatest concerns of buyers of products using new technology are often technical.

But as products mature, price, support, service, and reliability become more important.

We've seen the same progression in the management of high-technology companies.

The founders and first managers of most high-technology companies are engineers or other highly technical people. They typically have an expertise or invention, and create a company to build and sell it (but rarely to first perfect it — that's usually forgotten in the first planning — or to support it, which is also considered a headache at best).

With time, these founders either learn to manage, are replaced, fail, or compromise their expectations. Likewise, they learn to make their products efficiently or else their companies never get anywhere.

But once the management and manufacturing problems are solved, most companies realize that they need more help in marketing.

The natural inclination for many has been to turn to the only "experts" in marketing they know, those with experience at marketing-oriented consumer products companies. We've seen a huge influx of people from product brand-oriented firms into the computer business, for example, where they try to sell computers like they would sell a bar of soap or a six-pack of beer.

The best of these people apply the principles of marketing, studying both their customers and their competition, in addition to their own companies' characteristics. Unfortunately, many of these marketers haven't truly understood the difference between the motives of buyers of household products and those of business and industrial productivity tools. There is obviously a strong emotional content involved in many business purchases, but there is also a significant rational component.

If you define marketing as understanding the needs of customers and satisfying them, many companies have done an excellent job in the past, in diverse fields ranging from semiconductors to computers. Certainly the best semiconductor companies, though based in technology, spawned excellent marketers. Likewise, IBM was and remains an excellent marketing firm. Others in the industry have recognized this in fighting to hire graduates of Intel U., AMD U., and IBM U.

Ironically, as companies improve their marketing, they realize the importance of customers, and the importance of excellent communication with those customers. The result is an increasing emphasis on direct sales as opposed to resellers. This too is in contrast to consumer marketing, which is rarely direct (Avon being a rare successful counter example).

I've noticed a great concern lately about sales among

companies that gave it little attention in the past, figuring their products would basically sell themselves. In line with this is an increasing amount of attention to customer support. This is clearly a trend that could help firms strongly differentiate themselves from their competitors.

High-technology marketing differs from other marketing in a number of ways: its need to address credibility, its technical content, and the complexity of its products and messages. A sound grounding in other marketing techniques helps, but none of us needs to defer automatically to the "classic" Procter & Gamble-type marketers. They do well in their world, but do not excel in ours.

August 1988

Market in Downturns

Many computer and electronics marketers are starting to think that it's time to run for the trenches. They feel besieged on every front.

Starting with the semiconductor industry (which wishes it never had started publishing its book-to-bill ratio), the economy's growth has slowed. And as sure as night follows day, semiconductor industry slumps are followed by bad times for customers.

Excessive competition exists in almost every segment of the industry, partly a legacy of overly optimistic market projections and a surplus of venture investment.

And then there's IBM. Freed from its past antitrust shackles, the ungentle giant is wreaking havoc in every segment of the electronics and computer industry, both by actuality and anticipation. Look at IBM's victims.

Plug-compatible mainframe computers. Only Amdahl/Fujitsu and Hitachi/National Advanced Systems (NAS) are still competing, and NAS isn't making its own computers anymore. Itel, Storage Technology (STC), Philips/Two Pi, Trilogy Systems, and Magnuson Computer Systems have all given up.

Plug-compatible mainframe peripherals. The latest to throw in the towels are Control Data and STC, the latter through bankruptcy.

Engineering and scientific computers. Digital Equipment, Prime Computer, Harris, Perkin-Elmer, and Hewlett-

Packard are all feeling the heat as IBM's superminis gain increasing acceptance and its PCs find more uses on engineering desktops.

Small-business computers. IBM is pinching the market from the bottom with its ugly but capable AT and from the top with new aggressiveness in its micro/minicomputers, creating severe problems for Northstar, TeleVideo Systems, Durango Systems, Fortune Systems, Molecular Computer, Altos Computer Systems, and even AT&T. Exxon is only the latest to call it quits.

Personal computers. Victor Technologies, Eagle Computer, Osborne Computer, Hyperion, and Otrona are only a few that filed for bankruptcy.

Personal-computer software vendors. Competition and scarce management talent and resources were already hurting most companies even before IBM stomped on the market. Who knows what happens next?

Retailers and Chains. IBM already sells many of its PCs directly. What happens if it takes more in-house or adds mass merchandisers to the computer specialty stores it now uses?

So how can a company survive?

Given the virtual impossibility for most firms of raising money through the soft public and private market, the first inclination is to cut back: lower expenses, reduce staff, abandon expansion. The second inclination is to consolidate. And the third is to seek a safe haven.

Let's look at these options in order.

Cutting back selectively may not only be smart, it may be vital. The wrong things to cut are product development and marketing, the keys to the future of any company. The right things are often physical plants and personnel, but that's hard, both for the personal heartbreak and heavy commitments.

Another survival technique is consolidation. This, of course, is hardly new. Many of the small microcomputer and personal computer hardware and software makers are for sale - and at very attractive prices.

Needless to say, consolidation through merger makes a great deal of sense - if the resulting combination is truly stronger. Says a venture capitalist about to lose his shirt (or at least a sock) in one company, "Even the genetic engineering firms aren't trying to make a racehorse out of two dogs." But it may be the only hope, even if it's a questionable one.

One of the better strategies for survival is the "safe haven." Some niches in specific industries or job functions are waiting to be developed while others may result from new technology. None, however, are easy to find.

For most, a "complement-IBM" strategy is safest. It's amazing to see companies developing non-compatible proprietary workstations at a great expense, when they would be better off taking advantage of the acceptance IBM and UNIX have already gained and concentrating on the value that can be added.

There are tough times ahead. It's time to step decisively but nimbly, while avoiding being stepped on in the process.

February 1985

PUBLIC RELATIONS
STRATEGIES

Develop A Public Relations Strategy

In the past, these columns have covered many subjects related to marketing and public relations. They have included discussions of a number of public relations strategies, though they weren't necessarily highlighted as such.

I'd now like to start a series of columns, each focusing on a single public relations strategy.

Before discussing public relations strategy, however, it's worth a moment to review what objectives, strategies, and tactics are. Objectives are the conditions we'd like to exist. They're expressed as nouns. Strategies are the long-term actions to create those conditions, usually expressed as verbs. Tactics are the short-term steps required to implement a strategy, again expressed as verbs.

There's widespread confusion about corporate, marketing, and communications/public relations strategies. This is hardly surprising considering the technical backgrounds of many in the computer and electronics industries.

I've been able to uncover only three successful basic corporate (or perhaps divisional) strategies in the computer and electronics business: being the low cost supplier, innovation, and exploiting market niches.

There are many marketing strategies that support these corporate strategies, including product innovation, distribution innovation, geographic expansion, market segmentation, creating a market niche, and strategic alliances, among others.

Likewise, there are many public relations strategies that complement these overall marketing strategies. In most cases, companies use more than one public relations strategy to support their objectives. Among the 30 or more that I've collected some excel in power and versatility. Others fit narrower tasks.

Some of the most widely applicable public relations strategies are positioning, defining a market, setting a standard, building credibility, and gaining awareness. The latter is the most widely practiced and best known form of public relations. Many in the industry don't realize that it's only a part of public relations, though an important part.

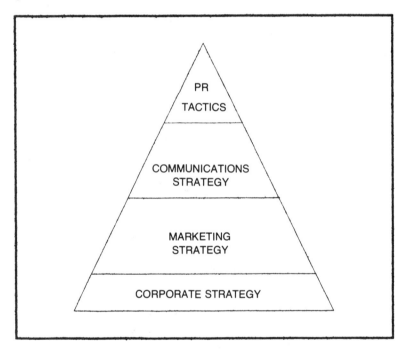

In all cases, public relations strategy follows marketing strategy. Before deciding on a strategy it's important to set objectives, measurable ones if possible. For example, if a company's marketing strategy is to create a market niche, its public relations objectives would likely include convincing potential customers that the niche exists, is viable, and is important to them. The best measurement of public relations success in this case would probably be objective studies before and after the process begins, but there are many other specific objectives that can be measured: successful completion of a product introduction, articles appearing in key publications, reports published by important analysts, and well attended seminars or meetings, for example.

The public relations strategies that support these goals might include defining and publicizing the market, building a technical reputation, and gaining credibility as a supplier.

Part of the process would likely include educating analysts, consultants, key members of the press, and other influential parties. Other "sub-strategies" would be customer references, publicizing strategic alliances, and most likely, an effective product introduction (a long-term process if it's to be successful).

Let's take a specific example, as I intend to do for future columns on public relations strategy. Most will be successes, but it's always interesting to look at some of the failures as well. Here's one.

Corvus was an early leader in local area networks for personal computers because it sold a simple-to-install, easy-to-use and low-cost, but versatile system called Omninet. Though limited in performance and versatility compared to other schemes, Omninet adequately served the needs of many users — notably elementary and secondary schools.

Unfortunately, Omninet was never considered a standard in the industry, and wasn't supported by other vendors. This was a big problem for Corvus, for another technology, Ethernet, was emerging as a standard. Ethernet was first promoted by Xerox, DEC and Intel, then by many other companies such as 3Com and Ungermann-Bass, and became the de facto standard of the industry.

Because of this, Corvus started losing visibility and market share.

Fortunately, the company was developing a new version of Omninet that offered many technical and economic advantages. The system was based on a chip made by NEC, one of the largest and most credible suppliers in the industry. This suggested a viable strategy to promote Omninet II as a standard. It would be an alternative standard, of course, but the local area network market abounds with standards. And the product did offer a number of attractive features to potential users.

Given that overall strategy, a number of substrategies and tactics appeared appropriate, including an elaborate introduction, complete with technical articles on the product, its development and its application. This would be part of an overall program to promote the company's technical reputation. Though little recognized for its expertise, Corvus had developed many innovative products.

A key part of the process would be to involve NEC and sign up third parties who would add credibility. Having OEM customers was vital. Finally, the company needed strong dealer and vertical market programs, and a product review program, a headache for LANs, but a necessity.

It would be great to say that the program was wildly successful, but it was never implemented, partly because of changes in the firm and its management.

July 1987

Position Your Firm or Its Products

$\mathbf{F}$or years, non-technical people working in technical fields have borrowed technical jargon for non-technical concepts. "Input" and "interface" are two that spring to mind.

Now, they're borrowing chic marketing jargon, often with little more understanding of the meanings of these words than they have of computer buzzwords. In particular, people in Silicon Valley are "positioning" everything. People. Products. Companies. Even lunches and meetings. As a result, a very important concept borrowed from consumer advertising is losing its meaning and, with this confusion, we may be losing an important marketing tool.

Positioning, as most marketers know, involves establishing a clear (and favorable) differentiation from your competitors in the minds of your customers. It's an ongoing process that involves not only well-directed public relations efforts, but also advertising, collateral, sales and promotion.

Part of that ongoing process is determining a desirable position for a company, but some people are confusing this consultation with results — achieving a favorable image. A good example is the Convergent Technologies Workslate, which failed in the marketplace. The Workslate is a clever product, offering some functions of a hand-held computer but missing a key feature: user programmability. Its marketing team correctly decided on trying to position it as a unique product, not a computer. Unfortunately, the implementation was inadequate. Most articles on the problems of the Workslate have mentioned the failure of the firm to communicate this difference.

Many observers attributed the failure to Convergent's engineering/manufacturing orientation and lack of experience in consumer marketing. Some marketing consultants suggest that anyone can develop a simple exercise for "positioning" in a matter of hours. Surprisingly, no one has developed a computer program for such a purpose, though it wouldn't be enough. A fill-in-the-blanks process can't develop a satisfactorily desired position, though having an organized system can be very useful. It helps assure that the right questions are asked about a company, its products, its competition, and its markets.

Creativity plays a vital role in determining a desired position. The great consumer-marketing campaigns didn't result from turn-the-crank research, but from individuals who thought of great ideas. The research helped focus, and it also helped test the concepts. But it's creativity that made the difference.

The key element in this process, however, is experience, both in the process and, perhaps more significantly, in the markets served. No system can replace this vital element.

Fortunately, many technology-based products and companies are really different from their competitors. This can simplify both the consultation and the implementation in developing a desired position, but it's vital to understand what the real difference is and make sure it's a strong differentiation that isn't easy to dislodge. For example, price (lower) and performance (better) are the easiest messages to communicate but also the easiest to topple: $1,195 instead of $1,295 or two nanoseconds instead of three.

Look at Osborne's or Kaypro's vulnerability in pricing, or the minor effect when instrument companies offer slightly better speed or capability, or a semiconductor firm announces a small improvement in access time.

As anyone can see, the computer and electronics markets are glutted with products such as microcomputer software, personal computers, semiconductors, and disk drives. The firms serving these markets face big challenges, since they must establish differentiation, in some cases artificially, and usually with inadequate funds.

Advanced Micro Devices established itself early on as a quality supplier, claiming military quality for all its products at a time when other semiconductor producers charged extra for this feature. AMD does have an excellent reputation, but it's not clear whether its products were actually superior to those from Motorola, Texas Instruments, and other suppliers.

In software, VisiCalc obviously had true differentiation but lost it to Lotus' better spreadsheet and stronger marketing effort. Perfect Software had good products, but those products got the reputation of having little value since they were bundled with a number of computers at no cost.

Remember that science has transmuted lead into gold and made silk purses out of sow's ears, but it was frightfully expensive to do so. That's the task facing some firms trying to market me-too products. Perfume and other consumer companies may spend half their revenues on establishing a strong brand awareness, but few markets for technology-based products will accept that price structure.

The strongest positions — quality, reliability, and support — are the most difficult to establish and take the longest. Clever marketers understand the strength of these positions but may underestimate the time, money, and experience required to establish them.

IBM, Hewlett-Packard, and Allen-Bradley, for example, have very strong positions that exceed their products, allowing them to sell against firms offering "better" products but less credibility.

Another common mistake made by inexperienced consultants is picking an untenable position for a company. A desired position must be credible. Picking an attractive position isn't enough. A *Fortune* magazine reporter recently mentioned the faux pas of a company that makes excellent low-cost ground stations for satellite communications. The company tried to convince the reporter that it was really a networking firm. Aside from the mistake of picking such a muddied and crowded position, the firm and its agency were trying to promote a position that no knowledgeable observers would accept and few business and trade reporters are ignorant.

Finally, it's worthwhile to remember that companies have positions in the market, but so do their products. And different audiences have different perceptions of the company and its products. It's vital to view these problems from many angles, again emphasizing the need for time and experience to do the job right.

Problems that occur when companies try to decide how they'd like to be seen in the market are one thing. Equally important is the need to communicate this desired position.

This is where good public relations implementation is vital. This is partly a function of knowledge of the public relations craft, but it's equally a function of the personality of the individual and agency doing the work. Motivation, intelligence, tenaciousness, hard work, and empathy are key. They are even more important than specific skills, at least when the individual is working in an agency where many people know the information and are willing to teach and share.

September 1984

Define a Market

Defining a market is a very important strategy for innovative high-technology companies. The subject of this column is Silicon Graphics Inc., supplier of engineering workstations that combine exquisite three-dimensional real-time graphics displays with excellent computing power. The products are used in sophisticated modeling, simulation, analysis and animation.

A few years ago, Silicon Graphics was one of many players in a confused and crowded market — engineering workstations used in computer-aided engineering (CAE). And whereas Silicon Graphics' products were primarily intended for demanding mechanical engineering applications, most observers considered engineering workstations synonymous with electronic design applications. This market was dominated by Sun, Apollo, and Daisy.

The strategy chosen to differentiate Silicon Graphics from the pack was to define a new segment of the workstation market, concentrating on the customer segments and applications. In this, Silicon Graphics would be positioned as the leader in the newly defined mechanical computer-aided engineering applications segment of the workstation market.

The tactics utilized to accomplish this effort were extensive. The first was to pick a name for the products — superworkstations. It was an obvious choice in retrospect, being descriptive and intuitive, patterned on supercomputers and supermicros. There was some opposition internally, however, since it seemed unsophisticated and "hypey." (It was, in fact.)

To support the claim that this was a distinct type of product, and that it served distinct markets, we prepared charts and tables that clearly differentiated Silicon Graphics' products from those of other players. One was a simple hierarchy of the products used in technical and scientific applications, with personal computers at the bottom, then engineering workstations, then superworkstations, minisupercomputers and finally supercomputers.

The chart also illustrated the big differences between the applications — engineering workstations were fine for two-dimensional electronic applications and two-dimensional mechanical applications, but not for three-dimensional mechanical design and simulation. This chart was clear even to the lay reporter.

CATEGORIES OF TECHNICAL COMPUTERS

Price	Vendor	Class	Application
$5 - 7 M	Cray-1 Cray-2	Super Computers	Massive Atmospheric Geophysical and Nuclear Simulation, Aerospace image Processing.
$0.5 M	Convex. Alliant	Mini-Supers	
$ 60 - 40k	**Silicon Graphics**	Super Workstations	3D Mechanical CAE (solids modeling)
$ 40 - 20k	Sun Apollo Dec Micro-VaxII	Engineering Workstations	2D Mechanical & Electronic CAD Drafting.
$ 15 - 5k	IBM PC/AT IBM RT/PC	Personal Workstations	Desktop Publiishing

Chart used in mid 1986 to help define super workstations.

Another table addressed technically sophisticated reporters and analysts, giving a comprehensive listing of the players, technical characteristics, and applications for the major segments.

The effort also required new background materials on the company. A white paper defining and explaining the markets and products and a new corporate presentation were prepared.

An important step in selling the concept of the super-workstation was pre-selling important market analysts who are widely quoted by the press as well as being influential on their own. These analysts included graphics experts, people from leading market research firms and financial analysts interested in the market.

After these briefings of analysts, we were able to refer them to the press for objective comments, though we naturally tried to refer those who seemed most positive.

This was followed by an intensive week of appointments with key editors and reporters at the National Computer Graphics Association conference, a leading show in the market.

Silicon Graphics also met with many other reporters who didn't attend that show.

In addition, the company initiated a customer/press newsletter called the *Superworkstation Times*, established a program to provide intensive support to its most influential editors and analysts, appeared at other important trade shows, created a series of well-attended seminars, and wrote technical and application articles.

One problem that arose in the process was that it was easy to define and promote the product niche (the super-workstation), but difficult to find a simple label for the markets served. As a result, there's more recognition for the product than the markets.

It was interesting to watch the acceptance of the term

superworkstation, beginning with the consultants and analysts, then the dedicated trade press, general trade press, then business and general press.

This is a fairly typical progression. A few years ago, however, the business press would often write an article about a new company in a new market. They were burned too often by companies and technologies that never became significant, so now tend to wait until a company has proven itself in the market (as Silicon Graphics has done) and in acceptance by customers, experts in the field and the trade press.

One measure of success of the program is that a number of companies have introduced products into this market in the last few months, and both they and the press referred to these products as superworkstations. It was gratifying to hear the president of Apollo, for example, introduce that company's new product as a superworkstation, comparing it to Silicon Graphics prominently in both his slide presentation and talk.

This process has helped analysts, press, customers, and potential investors better understand Silicon Graphics and its markets, and in so doing, has clearly established the firm as the leader in the field. Silicon Graphics' next challenge is to stay ahead of the recent pack of entrants into the market, both with technical and marketing innovation.

August 1987

Exploit Your Alliances

An important public relations and marketing strategy is alliance marketing. In fact, I think that you can make a good case for the (short) age we're in now being technology's "Age of Alliances."

It wasn't that long ago that the goal of every electronics based company was to become self-sufficient. "Vertical integration" was the catchword in the 70's, led by the prophet, Texas Instruments, Unfortunately, the prophet couldn't find profits in vertical integration.

Like TI, other companies in the electronics field thought they could best succeed by controlling every bit of their business, from manufacturing components (even materials and production equipment) to sales channels. Texas Instruments was the prime example with their belief that they could succeed even in consumer-end products if they did everything themselves.

Texas Imstruments even went so far as to own a chain of distributors, a technique guaranteed to discourage interest from leading independent distributors.

IBM and DEC espoused the same theory, establishing semiconductor manufacturing operations and even opening retail computer stores. The stores were subsequently closed.

In retrospect, it's clear that only the largest firms can justify such independence, and even they can benefit tremendously from long-term strategic cooperation with other companies. IBM maintains tight interdependence with Microsoft and Intel, for example, though few doubt that Big Blue could exist happily on its own.

For smaller companies, there is really no choice. I don't believe anyone can go it alone these days. They have to find partners that help them expand markets, save R&D resources, accelerate development, and reduce capital investment and sales and marketing expenses.

Alliances take many forms, from long-term vendor-reseller contracts to joint development efforts, to technology exchanges to manufacturing commitments. Examples are legion: Hewlett-Packard and Canon for laser printers, Software Publishing Corp. and IBM for software, 3Com and Microsoft for LAN systems software, Convergent and Unisys for computers, Altera and Intel, Cypress and WSI/Sharp for user-configurable integrated circuits.

Some companies haven't yet recognized the value of forming and promoting alliances. They still are embarrassed that they depend on other companies. They remind me of the companies I used to visit as a reporter 20 years ago. These firms always made it a point to show me their flow solder machine just to prove that they were real electronics companies.

I think it's clear that it's time to abandon that attitude and trumpet partnerships. They represent strength, not weakness, and both the press and customers recognize that.

Forming alliances is a basic marketing (and perhaps corporate) strategy. But exploiting them is equally an important public relations strategy.

Unfortunately, it's not always easy to exploit your alliances to promote strength and vitality. Everyone's favorite and worst partner is IBM. Favorite because it lends so much credibility. Worst because companies that get in bed with IBM have to be nimble to avoid being squashed.

In particular, IBM is famous for utilizing alliances solely

to its own benefit. It's rarely in Big Blue's interest to give other companies much credit — even if it gets key technologies from them. And it doesn't usually give much credit. It usually refuses to cooperate fully with other companies, for example, often approving news releases, if at all, with the speed of molasses.

And IBM won't usually come to your press conference or go on a press tour with you. Why should they?

.   This makes it extremely difficult for small companies to exploit their relationship with IBM for public relations purposes, leaving them to try to get permission to talk as much as possible on their own.

Fortunately, other partners benefit more from their alliances. Even major companies like Digital Equipment and Apple recognize the strength they lend to each other. As uncommunicative an executive as DEC's Ken Olson and as promotional a manager as Apple's John Scully were willing to get together recently to make a much bigger occasion than either could have done alone.

Announcements of this type involving at least one major player are naturals for press conferences, normally one of my least favorite public relations activities. Unlike major product announcements, these deals are best sprung on the press suddenly (though there's no question that leaks in advance increase interest).

One announcement doesn't make a public relations campaign, however. If an alliance is to be effectively promoted, it should involve other joint activities, including trade shows and seminars, road shows and jointly prepared literature and articles. And a campaign should include announcements of milestones that indicate progress.

Alliances demand effective public relations programs if they are to succeed. Fortunately, most alliances often add up to more than the sum of their parts in both marketing and public relations.

April 1988

Assert Technical Leadership

For most companies that sell to sophisticated audiences, being a leader in technology is a strong image. This is especially true for technical customers like engineers and data processing professionals, but it's equally true for many nontechnical markets. Mercedes Benz and innumerable Japanese camera and electronics companies have built whole businesses on their reputations for technical innovation and expertise.

To many companies, a reputation as an innovator is even more important in recruiting top people than it is in selling. Many firms that attempt to minimize their technical reputations to customers promote them heavily in their own industries to attract the best engineers. The help-wanted pages in the San Jose *Mercury News* and *Boston Globe* attest well to this.

Unfortunately, it's not easy to gain a reputation as an innovator. Like reputations for quality and reliability, a position as an innovator must be built on reality. The leaders in selling to engineers, whether for instruments like Tektronix, Hewlett-Packard or Mentor, or components like Intel, *are* technological leaders. They don't just *claim* to be.

But just as it's not enough to make claims, it's not enough to lead quietly and not tell anyone — unless you're prepared to wait a very long time for your leadership to diffuse through your markets. This has happened for HP and Tektronix, of course, but they have the advantage of very long histories in markets.

The methods used to shorten this process are fairly straightforward, but their impact is not immediate. For a company to be positioned as an innovator, it must make a long-term commitment to innovate and to promote that fact. Few firms do both.

Aside from commitment, the two secrets to communicating leadership are to publish (and present) extensive materials that illustrate this leadership — and to have other people say that you're a leader. The two processes go hand in hand.

Publishing technical papers seems simple enough, but few companies do it effectively. The first problem is normally lack of commitment and planning. For a process as strategic as this, a company should plan and budget to make sure that enough of the right types of articles and papers are written, preferably by the right people. You can't leave it to the inclinations of engineers. Many of them will write the wrong things if left alone, since their first thought is to write material that will impress their peers (and potential future employers), not customers.

Often, the "right" author is too busy, a poor writer, or not committed enough. In this case, the options are to use another qualified author, who could share the authorship, or hire a ghost writer. These people, many of them former journalists, typically charge $2,500 to $6,000 to write articles, often a bargain for the return.

Articles can be about new technology, major new products or applications of products. All contribute to the name of a company, and the latter two help sell specific products as well.

One especially prestigious type of article is the invited piece that surveys a technology. After all, no respectable publication would invite someone who wasn't a leader to participate. Commercial magazines rarely publish these articles, preferring to write them in-house, but organization journals do and they make great reprints.

Likewise, tutorial pieces, perhaps in magazines in industries served by your company (not in those read by your competitors) are very effective. Again, leaders teach. Followers don't.

It's great if your customers write articles about your firm and its products, even if you have to encourage them, pay for the writing, or do it together.

Guest editorials and columns are always prestigious and rarely occur by chance. They usually come from well-planned meetings and inquiries.

Speaking at conferences is a very important part of asserting technological leadership. Giving keynote speeches and invited papers are the ideal positions, but third best is organizing and moderating sessions where you can control the topic and invite the optimum speakers — preferably including customers or other third parties for credibility. Giving a paper itself is also useful.

The above suggestions are ways to publish and present material that asserts your company's lead. Equally important, and intertwined in the above process, is having other people say you're a leader.

Writing and presenting is one important part of this process. Reporters, editors and analysts read — or at least scan — their competition. They know when something is happening, particularly if they're missing something important.

The other key element in building a reputation as a technical leader is to develop relationships with influential editors and other observers, and help educate them about developments in technology and in the market. There are many ways to do this, but the minimum is to meet the key local and headquarters editors regularly. It's a good idea to organize a formal press tour regularly to make sure this happens.

One part of meeting with the press is to provide them with helpful background materials, both text and graphics. Though this material is rarely printed verbatim, it often inspires editors and can help promote your views and innovation.

All these steps will help assert technological leadership, but they won't do much good unless they're based on true leadership, and they're part of an extended program. A follower can't convince people it's a leader, but a leader doesn't appear one unless it tells people.

October 1987

Manage Word-of-Mouth

Numerous studies have demonstrated that word of mouth is the single most significant factor in choosing personal computer products. For that reason, it's vital to include word-of-mouth management in any public relations campaign for personal computer software or hardware.

Fortunately, it isn't too difficult to understand this process, though its implementation can be demanding.

The "mouth" in question belongs to the local expert, that person who always seems to know more about products than anyone else.

Some of these local experts are really knowledgeable. Just as it makes sense to ask a dentist you meet at a cocktail party about tartar-control toothpaste, or a refrigerator repairman about the reliability of the fridge you might buy, people who work intensively and professionally in personal computers should be good sources of information.

Likewise, the user of the product should give honest references — one reason that it's essential to make good, reliable, well documented, bug-free products, and to support them well. In fact, the word of mouth that emerges from this process is the most credible and effective, as Apple has demonstrated so well with its best products — the Apple II, the present Macintosh and the Laserwriter.

From a buyer's viewpoint, these real experts and present users are the best sources of information. Unfortunately, from the vendor's point of view, it's harder to manage the perceptions of real experts and users than those self-appointed experts whose knowledge comes largely from their interest, not their experience. And you can't use word of mouth to promote a bad product.

Too much of the process starts with better products validated by true experts. Nevertheless, it's a rare personal computer product, even an excellent one, that makes it without strong grassroots support.

Now let's look at the specific parts of a campaign that can help you manage word of mouth.

First, you should release plenty of technological news. The people who like to be experts are interested in innovation. They *have* to be in the know, and not just about me-too products. Fortunately, many enthusiast publications report news about technology, notably in their front-of-book sections.

Second, try to get your company or product featured in articles in serious consumer nut magazines. All the PC publications claim that they're read by corporate executives and buyers, but most have huge numbers of readers who buy the magazines mostly because of their personal interest. And many of these readers also influence the corporations that they work for.

While the casual reader is most likely to pick up popular and accessible magazines, the serious audience is often best reached via the more technical and esoteric publications, like *Byte*.

Newsletters and on-line data bases are also great sources of inside information, and so deserve the attention of companies wanting to spread the word to serious enthusiasts.

A lot of the articles in these techie publications are staff-written, but there are some opportunities for technical articles from authorities who happen to work for vendors. It's also possible to commission respected free-lance writers to do articles on subjects of interest.

Good reviews are obviously a key part of a word-of-mouth campaign. They're hard to program, however. Even if you have a great product, someone else's may be better. Or the reviewer may have certain prejudices.

In addition, some publications such as *Consumer Reports* have a counter-culture orientation that often leads them to pick a product that isn't the obvious choice, such as one from an unknown company.

Other publications tend to go with the big names. This may be because this is a safe approach, or because the big companies are more likely to be around and able to support their products, or even, sad to say, because of advertising considerations.

In general, in fact, the more obscure, specialized and technical the publication, the better for purposes of reaching computer cognoscenti.

Other ways to reach local experts who provide the channels for word of mouth are through users' groups, computer clubs, computer shows, and specialized conferences.

Users' groups are composed of the biggest potential proponents for any product. Normal consumers don't join product-oriented groups— those who are very committed do. That means manufacturers should do all they can to support these groups, an investment that pays off handsomely.

Likewise, computer clubs are full of people who are very interested in computers and new developments.

The influence of computer user organizations has undoubtedly dropped from the days when Steve Wozniak and Steve Jobs sold their first Apple computers as circuit boards at a club, but some are still important. In particular, the Boston Computer Society has intense and widespread influence.

Finally, computer user conferences and shows can be

very important in influencing self-styled experts. Again, a casually interested person isn't likely to go sit and listen to a bunch of technical and product experts talk about the subtleties of operating systems and memory expansion, but plenty of people do find it fascinating. They can be important to you if you're willing to reach out to them by providing speakers, literature, attention and advice.

In summary, word of mouth can be a most effective means of promoting a semi-consumer product like personal computers and software. And the process can be managed — but it takes planning and commitment.

July 1988

Promote an Issue

Issue-oriented public relations is rarely mentioned in the same breath with marketing products and companies, but promoting issues can be an effective public relations strategy.

Issues can be of many types. Compatibility standards are one type of issue, and promoting standards has proven a very successful strategy for many companies.

An excellent example of promoting standards is the effort companies have put into promoting Unix. Unfortunately for users, however, there seem to be as many versons of Unix as there are users.

Unix is a great issue. It seemed to offer many advantages to users: independence from proprietary hardware; a wide range of software from many sources; support from leading companies; acceptance in academia with the resulting base of knowledgeable and enthusiastic users.

Unix has always been a bit fragmented, however. The situation has become even more murky of late, with several major camps arising with the true form of Unix.

Nevertheless, companies such as Altos and AT&T have promoted Unix successfully.

Another issue is definitions of performance. A few years ago, for example, there was little appreciation among engineers of the importance of access time as a differentiator among disk drives. The discussions in magazines were always about capacity. Atasi, a company that made relatively expensive disk drives with fast access times, initiated a program to sensitize the market to the importance of speed, helping distinguish it from companies producing slower drives.

A third example of promoting an issue was the joint effort by Hewlett-Packard and Sony to encourage the industry to standardize on the 3.5 inch hard-shell "floppy" disks developed by Sony, and now the standard for new applications.

At the time, HP was introducing a personal computer using these disks. The disks were clearly superior technically, a feature HP always tries to incorporate in its products. Nonetheless, HP encountered considerable resistance from an industry that uses 5.25-inch disks.

In addition, a number of competing formats were fighting for acceptance as the next standard in the smaller drives everyone knew were coming. These included 3-inch, 3.5-inch and 100-millimeter (3.9-inch) versions of the existing 5.25-inch disk. All were smaller, but had no other advantages over the current standard. The 3.5-inch Sony format did, including ruggedness and high capacity.

Sensing the resistance, HP and Sony commissioned a program to illuminate the issue and, they hoped, convince the press and market research community that the 3.5-inch drive was the best solution for future drives. By implication, this meant that HP's personal computer was the forerunner of future products.

The program included a compelling white paper, a presentation on the subject, a tour by HP and Sony experts to influential publications and analysts, product reviews and mass mailings of the disk with promotional material.

The white paper was a key part of the program. It was a very reasoned and fair treatment of the subject, not a sales promotion piece. It was the type of article, in fact, that many publications publish. A few magazines even ran it verbatim, though that wasn't the intention of writing it. In all, the issue received a great deal of attention from the press, with many publications concluding the 3.5-inch disks were superior.

With all this attention, any lingering questions in the minds of the press about the issue were answered by Apple's adoption of the format on its Macintosh shortly after the program ended. The other formats disappeared.

A final issue was the safety of video display terminals. This was a political issue in California, but could have had a serious impact on the marketing of these products in one of the largest markets in the world.

As often happens, this issue arose because labor unions were attempting to organize office workers and seized on questions about VDTs to gain attention, and, they hoped, support from potential members. (The same type of campaign has occurred with health issues for semiconductor workers.) In both cases, there was some justification. For office workers, however, the real health hazards were eye strain and back and neck problems caused by poor posture. The most emotional accusations, claims about radiation and birth defects, were more controversial.

Nevertheless, the campaign created great concern and attention, and appeared that it could have serious impact on companies that make or market any type of product using VDTs. Today, that's most of the computer and electronics industry.

Fortunately, makers of VDTs and computer systems that depended on them initiated a program to counteract the unions. It focused on the state legislature and administration, where technically naive individuals were introducing and advocating unreasonable and damaging laws and administrative rules.

The program also included an educational campaign to tell users the facts about how VDTs can cause problems, and help the users avoid problems.

The lobbying was partly conducted by the American Electronics Association and other industry organizations better equipped for lobbying than individual companies.

The result: the issue died down and manufacturers were able to market their products without fear that they would suddenly be stuck with "illegal" terminals in their warehouses or in development.

Many other issues have helped or hurt companies market their computer products. Exploiting these issues is a valid strategy often overlooked by companies used to only promoting products.

June 1988

Set A Standard For
High Tech Products

E stablishing a product, or part of a product, as a standard is an important and effective marketing strategy. It has been used successfully by many companies and groups of companies in businesses as varied as semiconductors, computers, software, test systems and communications.

Examples of standard-setting products are legion: the first practical operational amplifier, the 709 from Fairchild; the first practical dynamic random access memory, the 1-kilobit Intel 1103; the 5.25-inch floppy disk standard from Shugart, IBM and Apple; the 3.5-inch hard-shell floppy disk by Sony and Hewlett-Packard; the RS-232-C serial asynchronous interface and the Centronics parallel interface for printers; MS-DOS from IBM and Microsoft; UNIX from AT&T; the PC, AT and Micro Channel busses from IBM.

Some of these standards were more successful than others. Some became standards almost by chance, without a specific campaign. But since these products first appeared, the world has become more complex. It's now increasingly difficult for a standard to just appear and be accepted.

Creating a standard is not just a public relations effort. It is, in fact, a basic marketing strategy that requires commitment. It involves far more than simply sending a message.

The first rule for a company that wants to establish a standard is to evaluate carefully. You can't establish a standard for a product that doesn't deserve it. The product, or interface, must be widely applicable, of interest to a diverse group and open to other suppliers.

Conversely, having a product with the potential to become a standard doesn't establish it as such. It usually takes a dedicated effort, most often by a leading supplier, but occasionally by an association or an interest group.

Setting a standard requires commitment by both your engineering and marketing departments. But at the same time, it's vital to assign responsibility for promoting the standard to one strongly dedicated individual in your firm.

Considerable time and resources are also required, and any company proposing a standard must first be willing to perfect it, then publish specifications, license the product (perhaps at a nominal cost), and then promote it heavily. Otherwise, it may never become established — unless the need is so overwhelming that customers or the industry demand it.

The company must also sign up partners, ideally some major firms, in advance of any announcement of intent to establish a standard. It's also imperative to develop and exploit alliances with OEMs, ISVs, customers, competitors and vendors.

A key strategy is formation of a committee to give credibility to the product. This can be done under the auspices of a technical or professional organization. But be warned that these groups can get out of control and reject the standard you're proposing. Or in the sense of "fairness," they can modify it in a way that destroys the competitive advantage of creating the standard. It's usually better to establish the standard first, then use a formal, "authorized" committee to enhance its credibility.

Another important tactic is to make a highly visible announcement of the standard. Depending on the subject and breadth of interest, this could be at a national press conference in New York or a press conference at a major relevant trade show. It certainly should include media saturation, beginning with a major article in a key industry publication (perhaps with a cover) and almost simultaneous articles in other important publications. A traditional — and excellent — place for these articles is in *Electronics*, which is well read by technology-oriented executives at computer and electronics companies.

Needless to say, the media coverage should include partners, particularly those prominent firms that lend credibility, and key customers who should be available and prepared to talk to the press. Brief appropriate analysts and consultants on the situation so they can act as references for the media. (Don't use them as references, of course, if you find out they're skeptical or negative!)

There are a number of materials you can use to help set your product up as an industry standard. A technical document defines the standard, and data sheets back it up. A "white paper," accompanied by a presentation, establishes the need for the standard and discusses user and industry benefits. Articles written by you or someone in your company — guest columns and editorials, how-to-use-it articles and papers, stories jointly written with customers or partners — get the information out to a wider audience. You should also put out announcements of additional acceptance, partners and customers.

A series of seminars, conferences, reviews and demonstrations gives you the chance to make face-to-face contact with your audience. Advertising, point-of-purchase programs and end user brochures, if appropriate, continue the chain of communication to the final purchase.

It's most important to remember that setting a standard requires a commitment to a continuing program of communications, not just a one-shot effort. Announcing a "standard" and then abandoning it almost guarantees failure. To effectively set a standard requires an ongoing marketing strategy that public relations can strongly support. A good standard can be a company's annuity, but it's easy to lose without effective work and followup.

September 1988

Use Well-Respected Influencers

When most people think of public relations, including many public relations professionals, they immediately think of the press. The basic tool, if you will, of most public relations programs is communicating with desired audiences through the media.

Of course, there are many media, and it's important to carefully analyze the best and most likely publications for any message. But it's vital not to forget the importance of another whole world of influencers, many of whom are as important for their impact on the press as on their immediate audiences.

The most influential people in the market might be independent consultants, individuals at market research firms, Wall Street analysts, professors, executives at key customer companies, or even members of the press themselves.

These people are important because they influence the opinions of others. It's sort of the global version of the way so many people buy VCRs, personal computers or cars: they listen to a friend or co-worker who seems to know a lot about the subject.

And where do those local experts get their opinions? In most cases, from reading special-interest publications, either consumer-oriented magazines or trade publications. Many also belong to enthusiast or industry organizations. Some even have hands-on experience.

To use the influencers on the press, it's important to first identify them. It's not that difficult in a specific field; what is hard is finding some general pattern that makes it easy to locate the key individuals in a new market.

The only way I know to locate the key influencers is to do some research. It doesn't have to be extensive in most cases. Just look at who is quoted in key publications, for example. Most magazines try to heighten their credibility by quoting experts; these same people often write articles, columns and guest editorials. Generally, the ones quoted or featured in articles have the most credibility.

Here are some specific influencers. The personal-computer market is not as hot as it was a few years back. And some of the people who were most quoted then have lost some of their shine.

Esther Dyson, one of the more insightful observers, seems to be focusing on subjects like artificial intelligence and other esoterics that may have vast impact in the future.

It's much like the transition of the predecessor of her newsletter. Those who've been around a while can remember when Ben Rosen's newsletter and conferences concentrated on semiconductors; Ben had jumped into the more topical personal computer at just the right time, as semiconductors were losing their bloom and PCs were beginning to flourish. Ben, in fact, remains one of the more influential people in the whole high-tech community, both because he has proved to be such a successful prophet through changes in the industry and because he has been so successful with his investments.

Who else has credibility in the PC area? Lots of people, from the looks of those I see quoted in the trade and business press. One interesting sign of the industry's maturity is that successful dealers and major customers seem to be getting more play than independent consultants.

In another high-tech arena, office automation, such long-time experts as Amy Wohl (Amy Wohl Associates of

Bala Cynwyd, PA) and Patricial Seybold (*Seybold Report* in Boston) remain prominent, partly because their individual direct consulting with clients keeps them on track.

In semiconductors, most market-research firms and trade organizations don't have proven experts at predicting the future, but they remain important for historic data. Jack Beedle at In-Stat in Phoenix gets good marks from most non-industry observers; he's not very optimistic, so the industry likes other forecasts better. Also in semiconductors, some Wall Street analysts are highly credible.

For disk-drive markets, Ray Freeman (Freeman Associates of Santa Barbara, CA) and Jim Porter (Disk/Trends of Los Altos, CA) remain most respected, again highlighting the desirability of specialization.

Likewise, Andy Rappaport (Technology Research Group in Boston) has gained enormous respect in semicustom integrated circuits and related electronic computer-aided engineering (CAE) in a short period of time.

These are only some of the key influencers in these fields. Six to ten typically dominate a market.

Having identified the key influencers, what do you do with them? Obviously, you send them releases, invite them to press functions and do all the other obvious steps. That's not where the secret lies. The secret is to involve them early, before anyone else knows what you're doing. Under non-disclosure, tell them what you're doing. They can provide a good reference to the value and importance of new products or strategy — though don't use them as references if they're negative!

So, there are the secret weapons of public relations. Amazingly easy, little utilized. As with other public relations tools, such as press conferences and road shows, they can be overdone, reducing their value to all of us.

June 1986

Differentiate Through Quality

Most public relations strategies aim for differentiation from competitors, but differentiation can take many forms. The most obvious are probably cost and performance, easy positions to establish and easy to dislodge.

The two strongest positions are probably customer support and quality/reliability. Both are difficult to establish, but harder to dislodge, especially so since they often go hand in hand.

Few computer and electronic companies have good reputations for customer service, but many are beginning to recognize its strength as a powerful marketing tool.

Customer support and quality are two strong public relations positions, but they well illustrate the necessity of tying a public relations strategy to a marketing strategy. Neither can succeed unless a company is willing to make a strong commitment that extends far beyond public relations campaigns. In a phrase, the company has to put its money where its mouth is. This is perhaps more true with quality and customer support than any other strategies.

Need I mention that the quality must be real? For many companies, this requires extensive and expensive changes in its attitudes and procedures, perhaps even its buying practices and test and burn-in processes. Worse, a company that is trying to develop a reputation for quality can't slip. Even one or two mistakes will blow the whole campaign. Fortunately, once a firm has a good reputation, it has more leeway; customers seem to be slow to abandon a good reputation built over a long period of time.

Once a firm really is making reliable, high quality products, it can then embark on a communications campaign to differentiate itself. This isn't easy. Quality and reliability are among the hardest virtues to promote, for most of the obvious promotional tools appear self-serving.

The difficulties a company encounters when attempting to promote these strategies are many. One is disbelief. What customers are so naive that they believe a company that advertises its high quality directly, for example? Advertising can be effective, but it must be a little subtle, even clever. Mercedes Benz has learned the lesson well. It doesn't claim reliability in its advertising. It proves it, notably by discussing engineering, test procedures, test results, racing wins, resale value and satisfied customers.

Many public relations techniques can, and in fact, must be used to support a quality-oriented campaign. Some, such as releases claiming quality, receive little pick up, but can make an impression. The most effective tools are customer and other third party references such as reviews, hard statistics, seminars and conference presentations, technical articles and papers outlining facts, real and unusual guarantees (not really a public relations technique, but a gutsy financial statement), and a personal commitment by a credible spokesperson such as Lee Iacocca.

In short, you can't claim quality. You must prove it, and that generally takes a long time, serious commitment and much good experience. It's rare that a company can short-circuit this process, but some have. I'll give two examples, neither of which I initiated.

In the mid '60s, Teradyne was attempting to establish itself as the leader in automatic test equipment for semiconductor products by clearly and controversially differentiating itself from other suppliers of test and measurement equipment. Traditionally, the biggest concern of anyone making measurements was accuracy and precision. Teradyne took another tack, claiming that reliability and throughput were most important in high volume production environments.

The company promoted its philosophy aggressively over a long period, using articles, brochures, ads, presentations and its president, an evangelical, controversial and articulate spokesperson. The approach was quite successful, and Teradyne succeeded in its aims, becoming a clear leader in its production equipment markets.

A second example of a company that has succeeded in building a quality image was Advanced Micro Devices. When AMD was founded in 1969, it had limited resources compared to not only its existing competitors but other start-ups such as Intel. The company started by second-sourcing other firms' products. This was a less expensive approach than developing new products, then developing the markets for these products, as Intel has done, for example.

Unfortunately, that left AMD with the problem of differentiating itself and its products from the competitors.

The company's president, Jerry Sanders, a former marketer at Fairchild, conceived a brilliant strategy. He decided to make all the company's products adhere to the demanding military standard for integrated circuits, even those designed for commercial applications. This appeared an expensive step, and it did cost the company a premium in manufacturing, qualification and testing, but AMD gained instant credibility and differentiation, and was often able to sell for higher prices in the bargain.

This approach worked well partly because everyone knew that AMD really had to meet the standards. In those days, no one messed around with government specifications, so this in effect was the ultimate third-party endorsement. Yet AMD could promote its quality freely without having to get customer permission, usually a big problem.

The result: AMD gained fast acceptance as a quality supplier, a reputation the firm has been able to maintain even though it has since undertaken other campaigns to add technological leadership to its image.

In summary, quality is a great public relations (and marketing) strategy. But it takes a heavy commitment and usually a long time to implement. It's an image that is becoming increasing important, so I suspect we'll see many firms attempting it in the future.

September 1987

Position Start-Ups
For Maximum Credibility

$\mathbf{N}$ew companies have different public relations needs than well-known, established firms. In a sense, they have an advantage: they start off fresh, with no preconceived, probably wrong images. But they have a difficult job establishing themselves in the minds of the press and their potential customers.

The tasks they face are visibility, credibility and communicating the correct position. The three can go together with careful planning and implementation, but they often don't.

For many companies, an ideal pattern is that followed by LSI Logic. This company, founded in 1981, has become a major force in the semiconductor business, but the way it did this is equally applicable to computer and other high-technology firms in other markets.

When Wilf Corrigan formed LSI Logic Corp., he wasn't sure what products he would make. He didn't know what technology he would use to make those products. He wasn't even certain how he'd get those products made. But he knew that there was a big opportunity in the electronics market and he intended to serve it and get rich in the process.

Corrigan should have known. Earlier, as president of Fairchild Semiconductor, once one of the leading innovators in integrated circuits, the controversial Corrigan had noticed that his firm and its competitors couldn't seem to satisfy certain vital requirements of their major customers.

Fairchild, like all its big competitors, was good at making standard products. They made these integrated circuits in huge quantities like jelly beans, an analogy so compelling that "jelly bean" was a common term in the industry for high-volume parts that engineers could buy off the shelf like bolts or hinges.

But many customers needed or wanted specially designed parts that only they could use, often in relatively small quantities. Big integrated circuit makers just couldn't seem to master this business. They could make and sell one million chips at 10 cents and make a profit. But they couldn't make only 10,000, sell them for $10 each, or even twice that, and make money.

Corrigan knew that he could succeed in this business. But first, he had to figure out exactly what the customers needed. Then he had to figure out how to supply what they needed. And finally, he had to communicate this information to potential customers.

One communications tool could do what Corrigan wanted. That tool was public relations.

The first step in public relations was to focus attention on LSI Logic's foundation. Since Corrigan was well-known, if unloved, in the electronics industry, the press was anxious to write about his plans. So a plan was developed, and materials prepared, that focused on the formation of the new company and its charter. Then the press was called.

Fortunately, there was much skepticism about the project, increasing interest in the new firm. Corrigan's reputation, and controversy over the viability of the niche Corrigan chose, helped the firm receive a great deal of attention without having to disclose specific plans.

Following this initial push, the firm's public relations focused on its resources, notably money (and its respected investors), newly hired executives and facilities. The company even announced the acquisition of a mainframe computer for design, a step that received surprising attention from the press at the time.

Perhaps most important, however, LSI Logic announced alliances with a number of other companies, one of the earliest attempts to really leverage the "strategic alliances" that have become so popular and important.

Through all this, LSI Logic acted like a big company in the making, not a niche player. Corrigan appeared on panels and was mentioned with the heads of Intel and Motorola, not the small gate array producers that had been laboring for years without great success.

All these announcements helped convince potential customers of the long-term viability of the company.

After about six months in business, LSI Logic felt comfortable discussing its technology. Its officers prepared papers, spoke at technical conferences, talked to the press about trends in technology, and released a constant stream of information aimed at increasing the technical credibility of the company. The publicity also had a desirable secondary benefit. It generated considerable feedback from potential customers, helping LSI Logic decide to focus on certain types of products.

Then LSI Logic introduced specific products, a moment of truth to technical reporters and editors. Fortunately, not only Corrigan but LSI's vice president of engineering, Rob Walker, knew of the importance of technical publicity in trade magazines. Walker had even run a public relations activity earlier in his career, making him unusually sensitive to this facet of his job.

Finally, a few years after its founding, LSI Logic could brag about its successes. The result: one of the largest initial public offerings in history, bringing Corrigan his success.

Corrigan and LSI Logic weren't alone in using public

relations to succeed in record time. Carefully orchestrated public relations campaigns have proven pivotal in the success of many other high-technology firms and their products. Microsoft, Apple Computer, Intel and Compaq are among other prominent companies that have marketed themselves, not just their products, through public relations.

This reliance on public relations contrasts strongly with traditional consumer marketing, where extensive and expensive advertising campaigns have made or broken most newly introduced products.

March 1988

Emerge from Bad Times

It looks like the long winter is ending for computer and electronics companies: it's not over yet, but conditions are definitely improving for the firms that didn't freeze or get eaten by the wolves during the recession.

Now it's time to look forward and establish a public relations strategy for the upturn.

The first thing to do is convince yourself and your company that things really are getting better. I know that it has been rough, but there are plenty of encouraging signs. If you don't believe times are getting better, it will be hard to act with conviction. So at the risk of sounding like a Mary Kay Cosmetics sales manager, I'd like to suggest a little pep rally to get everyone thinking positively and suggesting upbeat ideas. It may be the perfect first step toward moving ahead in an industry ready for some upbeat thinking.

The bad news is that it's hard to recover if you've stopped your public relations and other promotional activities during the bad times; the good news is that your competition has probably done the same. For that reason, a basic strategy is to stay ahead of the pack. Do things earlier and do them better.

The reason is simple: For most computer and electronics businesses — all businesses, for that matter — profitability is closely linked to market share and market share to share of mind. In the consumer business, it's a fundamental belief that share of mind precedes share of market, but that's something that's little appreciated by those in the high-tech field with an orientation toward technical excellence only.

Many companies neglect their images in poor times because of budget limitations, layoffs, and general cautiousness. As a result, it's fairly easy to beat them during a slowdown, and it's also easy to stay ahead of the pack on the way back. Big competitors tend to be ponderous, so the nimble players can make a lot of impact quickly, an impact that is hard to overcome except with much time and expense.

For that reason, this is the ideal time to introduce new products. It's also the ideal time to be aggressive in explaining new marketing directions and introducing new management players to members of the press, investors and customers. After all, public relations is the ongoing process of communicating messages to each of the audiences that comprise your network; it is definitely not a discrete event.

For products, the usual guidelines apply. Be the first to introduce an important new product, but make sure it's so good that competitors will have trouble one-upping you. And introduce it at the right time: when it's ready to sell for consumer products, early in the design cycle for OEM products and long in advance for major capital equipment that has a long selling cycle.

But don't be too early. Electronics and computer companies are famous for premature introductions and the resulting premature evaluations and premature rejections. Announce too soon and you're giving the competition time to steal some of your thunder and maybe all of your orders.

One caution, however, is to remember promotional tactics other than press-oriented public relations and advertising. If you're trying to make a splash in a short period of time, there are many other possibilities: direct mail, newsletter, collateral, seminars, trade shows, in-store promotions, and attention-getting mailings.

With the disappearance this year of dozens of computer magazines, existing publications have less available editorial space, making it more important to use creative tactics to get noticed.

Besides product introductions, it's important to begin the process (which I hope you never abandoned) of talking frequently to the press and other opinion makers on a continuing basis. This is essentially important to ensure that your firm has share of mine among editorial managers who decide what will be written and among trade-press journalists who regularly write and consult about your field.

You need to keep in touch with editors for two very important reasons: these people change jobs fairly often, and they are bombarded by attention seekers. Many influencers remember only the last few people who were in their offices, so it's important that you contact them on a regular basis.

So there you have some suggestions about how to emerge from hibernation and help shake off the chill. If you take a hard look at some of my suggestions, you'll find that I have focused on the basics: make decisions based on market research and customer requirements, educate influencers, plan timely product introductions and incorporate creative tactics to gain maximum attention. That's because sometimes it's extremely important to review the basic steps to achieving successful results, especially after a bad year.

March 1986

Use Public Relations on Marketers

D espite years of work in public relations, I've rarely heard a client suggest that sales and marketing people are key buying influences. Perhaps that's because clients are too close to that element, generally being marketing people themselves or marketing-oriented executives. That's ironic because the right marketing people can have a big impact on corporate buying decisions.

Marketing managers in general influence companies in three ways:

• Suggesting products that they believe will appeal to their customers.

• Promoting both the concept of strategic partnerships and specific partners.

• Controlling buys at companies such as banks and airlines where automated-teller networks or reservation centers may be vital parts of the marketing organization.

Marketers affect many major purchases by their employers. They also affect development of new products, which allows them to have an impact on purchases of components and sub-systems. But let's focus on their less noted influence on direct buys.

71

One important influence of marketing and sales people is their recognition of the value of key relationships with other companies. That can be as simple as choosing suppliers.

Marketing and sales people may want IBM personal computers or Digital Equipment Corp. minicomputers to be a visible part of their company's computer operation because of customer acceptance of these products and their vendors. They may even hope that the reputations of those respected companies will rub off on, or reflect well on, their lesser-known company.

The same is true of popular microprocessors and operating systems. Many engineers *know* that they could develop a better operating system, but no marketer would choose to face customers demanding 68000s and UNIX or 80386s and MS-DOS or OS/2. Why else would so many engineering and technical products be based on the IBM PC standard, for example. No one will claim that the PC is the best machine for this use — even IBM must think the RT is better — but that doesn't matter. Customers want it.

Other partnerships have great marketing value, too. Marketing and sales people obviously select distributors and other sales organizations. They also help choose service organizations, an increasingly vital factor in many purchases. In addition, they help pick suppliers of consumables and accessories that could be key elements of an overall program. Think of the frustration in trying to sell a printer without such key components as paper, ribbons, or hard-to-find cables.

One area in which marketers can have vast impact on purchases is rarely recognized by most people involved in marketing and sales: marketing departments control major computer and communications systems in many of the organizations in which they work.

At banks, retail-sales organizations, transportation companies and specialty marketing groups, information handling and processing systems are considered key competitive marketing advantages. As such, they are controlled by specialists in the marketing chain, not corporate MIS directors. That's true for such products as automatic teller machines, point-of-sale terminals, reservation systems, transaction-processing computer systems, communications networks, and sophisticated phone and inquiry-handling systems.

Fortunately, it's generally easy to reach the right marketers with public relations. The same cannot always be said of advertising to them, for they're often a relatively small segment of most magazines' circulations which can drive the cost per thousand to impractical levels. For public relations, on the other hand, the cost is lower and more related to the number of publications. It's just the likelihood of success that varies, not cost per key reader.

Fortunately, marketers, unlike many prospective customers, do read. Their need to keep up with competitors and their customers is much stronger than that of some other audiences, such as dealers, business end users and even some designers. That ensures your message will be noticed.

The three most effective channels to reach marketers are industry-specific publications, marketing publications, and general business and consumer publications.

Some typical industry-specific (i.e., vertical) publications include *Aviation Week, ABA Banking Journal, Electronic News* and *Computer Systems News*. This type of publication concentrates on industries, not functions. Ironically, industry-specific publications often try to minimize the numbers, or at least the acknowledgement, of these marketing readers since most advertisers aren't interested in reaching them.

Marketing publications are typical of horizontal, or functional, media. Some general ones include *ADWEEK* and *Business Marketing. Marketing Computers* is a hybrid, being a horizontal publication for a large collection of complementary vertical markets.

Also highly focused are specialized publications about technology for specific industries such as the *Wall Street Computer Review* and *Computers in Banking.* One would assume that they would be useful in reaching some of the key marketing prospects, but it would depend on how well the magazine serves the field.

The other group of media key to reaching marketers includes general business and consumer publications. The same considerations apply: it's not always easy to get coverage, particularly when many of these publications have de-emphasized their treatment of technical subjects. For that reason, it's best to focus on industry-specific media.

May 1986

Market via Wall Street

Along with the press, there are many other important influences on marketing efforts. The most prominent of these influences are market researchers and consultants. They have two major impacts: directly on potential customers and indirectly by influencing the business and trade press, which quote them to lend additional credibility to their articles or borrow their ideas expounded in reports, conferences and interviews.

Another group of influencers also gets significant attention from technology-oriented writers: financial analysts.

High-tech companies are now beginning to realize what more traditional industries have long recognized: the financial analyst is a credible, informed spokesperson. These people are often quoted by the trade and business press.

These analysts have been there all along, but a number of forces have recently tipped the scales of influence in their favor. These forces include consolidation in the market-research field and loss of credibility for some researchers as a result of bad predictions.

But perhaps as significant is an unstable stock market, which attracts extra attention to Wall Street.

In the realm of marketing products and services, some of these Wall Street analysts have a great deal of influence on customers, either directly or indirectly, just like the market-research firms.

What happened among market-oriented researchers that has helped Wall Street analysts move into the high-tech marketing spotlight? It's little secret that there has been major consolidation among market-research firms. Among those acquired were Yates, Future Computing and Software Access. In addition, a number of people have left the field with their companies disappearing with them.

Nevertheless, the major survivors, such as Dataquest, International Data Corp., and Gartner Group remain prominent and successful because they offer valuable and divergent services. And some individuals and small companies continue to provide excellent advice and data in specific market niches and industry segments.

The press will continue to quote these people, so it's vital to inform them of your company's position relative to such important elements as competition, markets, products, technology, strengths, and progress.

Few would question the importance of financial analysts on the valuation of stock; their impact on marketing is less noted but just as real. They are quoted by the trade and business press, and astute customers know that many analysts are exceptionally well informed about company direction and viability.

Some of these analysts are natural leaders, while others simply follow their lead. The best known include those at firms noted for underwriting initial public offerings of high-technology firms: Hambrecht & Quist; Montgomery Securities; Robertson Colman; and Alex. Brown & Sons. Major wire houses such as Prudential Bache, Shearson Lehman, Salomon Brothers and Merrill Lynch have many highly credible analysts. These firms have recently accelerated their interest in technology offerings. Examples of leading semiconductor analysts, for example, are Tom Kurlak at Merrill Lynch and Adam Cuhney at Kidder Peabody.

Most of these technology analysts are very knowledgeable, far more so than most of the reporters, editors and even market analysts we encounter. The typical financial analyst covers companies in a broad market segment. They have a good understanding of the technologies, products, management, customers and, obviously, financial performance.

You can find out who they are by noting who gets quoted in *The Wall Street Journal, The New York Times,* major general business magazines like *Forbes* and *Fortune,* specialized business magazines like *Computer Systems News, Electronic Business* and *Electronic News,* financial columns and radioTV broadcasts. Each year, *Institutional Investor* magazine rates the analysts, an important list worth obtaining.

These analysts tend to be very busy, skeptical and intolerant of incompetence. If you decide to talk to them, be sure to get your act together first. Be prepared and have a superb spokesperson and investor-relations professional involved. Don't expect much time from them unless you're a customer or have the potential of bringing some business to the firm.

In general, they have little interest in small divisions of large companies, which have little impact on the stock of the firm. They're also not very interested in private companies that aren't going to go public or be acquired any time soon or in companies that they've already written off as dogs.

Communicating with these analysts is much like communicating with the press or market analysts: it works best in person and at financial forums; next best is by phone, wire service or mail, in that order. Just be timely and aware of the legal and financial consequences of any communications.

Of course, it doesn't do much good to tell anyone your story unless they're going to do something with it. If you're public, their baby and hot, they'll take care of it, of course. If not, and you're sure that they understand your situation (and aren't negative), be sure to refer the press to these specific analysts.   *August 1986*

Get Good PR from Good Deeds

Computer and electronics companies have generally been very niggardly in donating to charitable, cultural and educational causes, at least compared to other firms in more established industries.

Perhaps one reason for this situation is the lack of tradition in these new fields and among their often newly-wealthy founders and managers. But it's equally likely that many of them haven't really understood the specific benefits that can result from involvement and contributions. These go beyond the obvious tax breaks, and extend to many significant public relations and other marketing benefits.

Some of the benefits relate to employee and community image, with their attendant recruiting appeal. These include creating an image for a company as a good place to work, and for its community a good place to live. In an area that is crowded with potential employers, well publicized activity can actually help create company visibility and differentiation.

More relevant to most high-tech marketers are the marketing benefits that can result from well-planned donations.

Companies that sell to the public — including some electronics and computer companies — have long been aware of the value of sponsoring visible charitable events, sometimes spending significant amounts of money on preparation and planning, publicizing and advertising these special events.

Macy's, a middle and upper-middle market department store, for example, recently persuaded more than a thousand persons to pay $50 each to see a fashion show in one of its locations in California and visit its newly upgraded facilities there, helping to move the store upscale in its battle to win over the upwardly mobile pocketbooks that had been opening increasingly at a nearby Nordstrom. The proceeds from the Macy's show went to a number of worthwhile causes, including the fund raising drive of the San Jose Children's Discovery Museum (of which I am a board member), but I suspect Macy's got a great deal of benefit from it too. To name just two benefits: lots of publicity before the opening, plus direct access to prospective customers.

Many computer companies could do the same thing, whether they sell directly to the public or to specialized markets. Some of the pitches involved can be subtle, but Macy's certainly wasn't. These events could even involve a plant opening; more typically, they would be held elsewhere, such as a museum, theater or other community facility.

Many firms sponsor exhibits at museums that reach their desired audiences too. The Boston Museum of Science, Boston Children's Museum, and Boston Computer Museum are three excellent examples, but there are many other opportunities around the country. Silicon Valley will soon have the Children's Discovery Museum, with exhibits sponsored by many companies, including Apple, with an obvious benefit to them. The High Technology Center of San Jose is also trying to raise money, some of it for similar exhibits.

A few firms, but more often their executives, have taken the big step of making major grants to universities or cultural organizations, sometimes getting their names on the buildings.

One of the most impressive examples in the computer business is Dr. An Wang's $4-million gift to Boston's ailing Metropolitan Center. It's now called the Wang Center for the Performing Arts, constantly reminding people of Wang Computer as well as Dr. Wang's generosity.

Cultural events can also build relationships with customers, prospects and others. Last year, my agency sponsored a performance of the San Jose Symphony with an attendant reception. The event attracted many people, such as corporate executives, who probably wouldn't have attended a simple open house that in total would have cost almost as much.

Again, a subtle or obvious pitch can be included, but in truth, sponsoring such an event places a company in a different category than one that just has parties at trade shows or holidays (not that those functions can't be useful).

One simple idea that seems to be implemented far too infrequently is to hold functions at cultural or educational institutions rather than at the usual hotel or restaurant. Many museums, for example, are excellent places for holding receptions and seminars. Most have meeting rooms, perhaps even auditoriums, suitable for either small or large groups.

A final good deed, which can repay itself mightily in publicity and future market development, is to donate to schools and other educational groups. Apple, with its extensive sales to elementary and secondary schools, is a leader in donations at this level, whereas IBM, Hewlett-Packard, and Digital Equipment Corp. all donate to universities and colleges. Aside from the value in preselling future or present customers, these high-tech companies also gain publicity for their gifts, a legitimate reward for their generosity.

Publicizing is a critical part of using good deeds to get good attention. It's admirable for a company to make donations in any event, but only good sense to tell people about them. There's a danger of backlash, however. It's unseemly to brag excessively about your good work, especially if it involves other people's hardships. I'd recommend publicizing gifts to community and educational causes, but keeping most charity private, except as needed to inspire others.

May 1987

Vertical PR:
More Than Just Press Relations

Press relations make up such a large part of most public relations programs that many people believe the two are one and the same.

But a solid PR program involves more than just press relations. Rarely is this more apparent than in the smaller vertical markets, those specific industry segments like optometry, industrial construction or hardware stores.

That doesn't mean that press isn't important in these specialized market segments, but depending solely on media in most niche markets is a ticket to failure.

In wider horizontal markets like engineering or office automation, the press is likely to reach and influence most potential customers. But in vertical markets, it's important to use a whole range of public relations tools. Let's take a look at how these tactics can help reach more exclusive segments.

What distinguishes vertical markets from wider ones is a sense of belonging. It's difficult to sell successfully in these small markets unless your firm — and in particular, its management — is accepted as part of the group. That means a much greater emphasis on personal contact, participation in local and national trade or professional organizations, and attendance at and participation in appropriate conferences.

This sense of belonging is easiest to accomplish if you

start that way. Many successful vertical market suppliers come out of the markets they serve. Printers start computer systems companies. Farmers develop devices that measure milk output from cows. Advertising agencies develop billing software (such as that used in our agency).

But if your company wasn't founded by someone from the field, next best is to hire visible representatives, notable sales or marketing people.

Your third choice is to develop expertise and rapport. It's especially vital for those who call on customers or attend trade shows to appear to be members of the clan.

You should have a solid presence at trade shows, but it's at least as important to join professional and trade associations if possible. It's also helpful to attend local trade-group meetings, perhaps sponsoring refreshments or entertainment.

Another important public relations tool to use in a vertical market is the seminar. Whether held locally at national conventions or just away from day-to-day work, seminars provide an excellent vehicle for targeted communication — and the chance to interact with customers in a favorable environment with a sense of belonging.

Those are the key non-press public relations tools for vertical markets. But despite the effectiveness of these methods, you shouldn't just write the press off. It is generally important in vertical markets, and every market I've ever encountered has its own media. Depending on the size of the segment, the media might be newsletters, trade magazines, professional journals, newspapers, or even radio and television programs or channels.

The level of professionalism in these types of publications varies widely. Some of them, notable professional journals like the *New England Journal of Medicine* or commercial trade newsweeklies such as *Aviation Week,* are as respected as any of the mainstream publications.

These magazines and newspapers play a vital role within their industries, both for their readers and the vendors seeking to serve the markets. Depending on the publication, the best opportunities for publicity include product announcements, tutorial articles by experts on your staff, case histories of how companies in the market use your products, interviews with experts and executives, and guest columns and editorials. In other words, the usual fodder of press-oriented public relations programs.

Two of these venues — tutorial articles and case histories — stand out in many of the smaller vertical markets.

Clearly written educational articles on how to choose and use computer products often appear in these magazines, helping their usually technically naive readers understand why they need these products. Educating readers in this way is an excellent method to build credibility. Everyone assumes that it's the leaders and true experts that teach, and writing educational articles reinforces this view.

The other opportunity that stands out in vertical publications is the case history. Many of these magazines have small staffs, and are happy to receive well-written, objective testimonials. It's important to inquire first, however. Some of the most influential publications prefer to write their own, have strict requirements or don't use case histories at all. As a result, there are hundreds of public relations agencies, corporations and free-lance writers laboring to write thousands of these applications articles that may never be used.

A final opportunity to reach vertical trade publications is to become part of the publication itself. There are two good possibilities here — as a member of the publication's editorial advisory board or as a columnist.

Not all magazines have advisory boards, but those that do normally pick recognized experts in the field they serve, often among vendors. This position usually takes little time, but is a good entree to the magazine and its readers.

Columnists have even better opportunities. A columnist has to be careful not to act too biased, particularly if he or she is to build credibility and attain longevity in the position. I should warn you, however, that writing a monthly column can be demanding, though the rewards are worthwhile.

In summary, the vertical trade press is certainly an important channel for influencing prospective customers, and other public relations techniques are equally — or more — crucial. But the most important public relations of all is to cultivate a sense of belonging to the market you serve.

May 1987

INTERNATIONAL

Public Relations in Japan

It's well known that most U.S. companies have a tough time selling their products in Japan. Even though many formal import restrictions have been lifted by the Japanese, informal trade barriers, language and cultural differences — and an ingrained "buy Japanese" attitude — conspire against foreign suppliers.

It seems that only big-name luxury goods and American fast foods attract the Japanese buyer. And it's unlikely that many of us are going to have the chance to sell J&B integrated circuits, Gucci oscilloscopes, or McComputers in Akihabara, Tokyo's amazing electronics bazaar.

The public relations scene only confirms the problem of sales and marketing. A recent trip to Tokyo crystalizes the challenges that U.S. companies face in publicity efforts in Japan.

The first problem is that public relations isn't recognized for its value in Japan as it is here. Public relations in Japan as part of strategic consulting seems little recognized because so many major and minor high technology companies are engineering oriented. Large companies in Japan have considerable clout, so they don't have to orchestrate elaborate PR strategies. Most PR is done by an in-house staff, while external agencies often provide publicity services — sometimes just printing and distribution and sometimes only as an adjunct to advertising clients. There are only a few high-tech specialists.

One difference is that daily newspapers are very important for disseminating significant technology news in Japan. The trade media is proportionately less important.

Newspapers have huge circulations and compete agres-
sively with one another. As a result, most companies try to
treat them impartially, often warning the press two days
before a major announcement. This action, in effect,
notifies the press that the company will not answer any
inquiries until the formal unveiling. In turn, the papers
don't publish information prematurely.

Release of information is made at conferences at a major
press club. Normally, only Japanese media are invited,
though there are a few exceptions.

Because there is a fairly steady turnover of reporters at
the major Japanese dailies, a company must educate reporters about the significance of the development. Thus, part
of any press conference is educational to make sure that
everyone understands the background and importance of a
new development. This is an often neglected yet vital task
for U.S. companies dealing with the press in Japan.

Because reporters change their beats so often, it's hard to
develop relationships with individual reporters. You don't
see experts like those in the U.S. press with decades of
experience in this particular area. Because of the different
structure of society, it's unlikely that a lowly reporter would
be granted access to high-level executives in Japan as they
are here. In Europe, where the same situation exists, it can
benefit U.S. companies with more democratic policies since
it seems to flatter reporters. In Japan, however, personal
interviews with presidents of big companies might upset
those companies' sense of order.

One of the fundamental results of this structure in Japan
is that the Japanese press is most interested in the significance of developments in technology. They want to hear
about breakthroughs, not product availability. Products are
often disclosed in what we would consider very early

stages. In the U.S., announcing a product long before it's available could have a serious impact on sales or existing products. In Japan, it's expected so that companies can plan ahead.

Since U.S. companies don't follow this practice, it can be a maddening dilemma: They appear to be lagging behind Japanese suppliers with new developments. It's obviously not practical for U.S. firms to announce products early in Japan hoping that U.S. publications will do a bad job of covering developments in Japan.

These comments apply somewhat to a huge company. What can smaller companies in Japan do to attract media attention?

For smaller companies, trade and special-interest consumer magazines are obviously of more practical importance than they are to big firms. And it's easier to develop personal relationships with the key people at these publications. Many of these publications are amazingly large — full of ads and in constant need of editorial material.

As in Europe, there is often a closer relationship between advertising and editorial coverage than is customary here. This is good, I suppose, if you advertise extensively; bad if you don't!

You'll note in Tokyo that many Japanese managers and journalists speak English, and even more read it. But it's obviously both polite and smart to have translations done by an expert in your field, preferably one residing in Japan or not long removed. We're all aware of the peculiar English that appears in some Japanese instruction manuals, and I'm assured that the same thing occurs in American documentation written in Japanese, although they're more polite about it than we are.

In general, cultural differences are as important as differences in public relations. Some study of Japanese social and business customs should be undertaken before embarking on any business venture in Japan. *August 1985*

Public Relations in Europe

The typical U.S. electronics or computer company sells about 30 percent of its products overseas, but it's often in spite of, not because of, its promotional activity.

Most American firms do a bad job of marketing their wares overseas. This isn't surprising. The United States has a long history of isolation from the rest of the world, and we still have an unwillingness to adapt to the ways of others.

That's certainly true in public relations. Even companies that do a great job of public relations in their home market often have trouble planning and executing well overseas. Many obstacles lead to this situation: distance, culture, language, and costs.

The typical approach for a smaller firm that sells overseas through national distributors is to let the distributor handle the job. Surprisingly enough, this often works well if the firm has the right distributor. Many of these companies understand their own markets well and have developed relationships with local public relations agencies or have good internal staffs. The only problem is that a company is likely to end up with great work in one or two countries and abysmal results in others.

Many companies are large enough to have their own staff members in Europe. They may or may not do well. Other firms use large international public relations agencies, which rarely specialize in high technology, or they deal independently with separate agencies from the U.S., a nightmare in logistics.

The basic problem with any of these schemes — and they all have problems — is that it's hard to overcome a fundamental problem: dealing with a number of different countries and cultures. Each is as complex as the U.S. market, yet each represents much lower sales. So, on a percentage basis, public relations is relatively expensive. It costs a lot for effective public relations (or any marketing activity) overseas - perhaps not as much per country as in the United States but close to it for an equal job, assuming all overall plans and materials are excluded from the equation.

Let's start with the good news. Foreign journalists seem much more interested in our news than do most U.S. writers. They pay more attention, ask more questions, spend more time, and write more copy. Some are rather sensationalistic compared with the staid U.S. press, hardly surprising if you pick up a copy of England's *Daily Mirror* and compare it to the *Washington Post*.

Inexperienced European executives sometimes think American journalists are rude and unresponsive, and they are very disappointed when their extensive remarks are greatly truncated or even ignored. But for much of Europe, what happens in the United States, especially in Silicon Valley, is big news even in national papers. And because European journalists rarely have the chance to meet informally with top U.S. executives, they seem to respond enthusiastically when American company presidents visit them. A press tour to Europe is a lot bigger ego boost for U.S. executives than one to New York, where even junior reporters at minor trade magazines try to act like they're the editors of *Fortune*.

But there are a lot of snares awaiting any U.S. company looking to expand business in Europe via public relations:

Lack of control over timing. for example, European journalists read *Electronic News* and *Computer Systems News;* they know if a company introduced a $399 product in the U.S. last year. So, it's hard to convince them that it's big news now and that the product is worth $999 just because the company is taking an airplane trip overseas.

Many European publications have full- or part-time correspondents in the United States, which only complicates the situation even more. Like East Coast-based American magazines that retain correspondents on the West Coast, these European publications have made an investment to serve their readers and want companies to recognize and use this network.

As anyone who deals with the international press corps knows, they have different attitudes about journalistic ethics than those practiced here. No leading U.S. newspapers or business magazines, and few major trade magazines, will accept the extensive travel and entertainment expected by many journalists from other countries. Part of the reason may be the smaller size and lower revenues of the foreign press, making it necessary for them to take freebies if they want to cover news.

Likewise, the wall between advertising and editorial doesn't seem as high in many markets as it is here. Being a major advertiser may help get attention from editors and reporters here, but it rarely has much effect on coverage at worthwhile publications. In Europe, there's often a direct relationship; it's easier to buy magazine covers — sometimes quite literally. Differences between the United States and foreign countries' publishing practices aren't necessarily huge problems if they are understood: Some companies would be delighted if getting a favorable article in *Forbes* or even *Electronic News* were as simple as paying someone off.

Differences exist not only between the United States and overseas but among foreign countries themselves. When to have press meetings, what day of the week, what time of day, and where to have meetings depends on the country. In France and England, most journalists are in Paris or London, but in West Germany there is no news center, making multiple locations mecessary for press announcements.

Then, there's the problem of translations. Many foreign journalists know English well, but most still prefer that we translate releases and articles for them. It's hard to blame them since that reduces their work tremendously. But it's hard to get good translators, particularly of technical material, documentation, manuals and sales collateral. It's best to use local ex-journalists familiar with the material.

July 1985

Public Relations in Canada

Most American high-tech marketers haven't quite figured out what to do about Canada. It's clearly a separate country and an attractive market for most U.S. computer and electronic firms, yet Canada just does not fit into a neat category for a U.S. firm's marketing, public relations or sales purposes.

If Canada were in Europe, it would probably be a little easier to deal with. Many U.S. firms have no problem dealing and doing business with smaller European countries, but Canada seems too small a market — even though it's physically large — to treat separately from the United States for most moderate or small companies. Yet Canada is geographically close and has a great deal in common with the United States. More to the point, it's the largest market for U.S. goods, even larger than Japan.

Most U.S. firms sell in Canada through subsidiaries or a few distributors. Both can work quite well. Other companies, however, try to treat Canada as if it were another state, a shortsighted approach which is almost guaranteed to fail.

Handling public relations in Canada is equally difficult. While Canada's market is about the size of a large U.S. state, the country is absolutely huge and diversified into four market regions.

The East, the first market, is English-speaking and headquartered in Toronto and Ottawa. Toronto is obviously the commercial center, and the location of most English-speaking publications. Ottawa, as the seat of government, is also important because of the relatively large impact of the government in the Canadian high technology economy.

Second is the French-speaking area, mostly Quebec. This particular market remains quite distinct from the rest of Canada. Ironically, French speakers, with their strong culture, are less concerned about U.S. dominance than the English speakers.

The third group to consider is the West. Western Canadians have some of the same feelings of separateness from their Eastern Canadian counterparts that American Midwesterners and Southerners feel toward U.S. Easterners.

Finally, Vancouver and much of British Columbia comprise an area which is almost like a mini-U.S.A.

Unfortunately, these regions don't generally have individual trade and special-interest magazines. Even more complicated, the computer and electronics buyer north of the border usually has some access to American publications.

That creates a problem, because Canadian products and prices must be comparable to the available U.S. versions. Canadians aren't going to be happy if they find that there's an unreasonable mark-up for a particular product, though they're quite realistic about customs, shipping, and the value of the Canadian dollar versus United States currency.

Even though American magazines have some circulation in Canada, Canada does have its own trade press. Just as in the United States, some publications are quite good in serving their markets. But U.S. business, for the most part, doesn't really know much about the Canadian trade press.

Two of Canada's better-known computer publications are *Canadian Datasystens* and *Computer Data*. The editor of *Computer Data* says that only a handful of U.S. companies really seem to realize that Canada needs to be treated as a unique entity. Not surprisingly, he finds that companies with Canadian subsidiaries tend to be much more sensitive to the needs of the Canadian market and its press. This is a view echoed by all those interviewed for this article.

The editor doesn't have too many gripes about the companies that work with him. The biggest problem he seems to have is getting information from U.S. companies in a timely manner.

An assistant editor at *Canadian Datasystems*, a magazine for data processing professionals, has more complaints about U.S. companies that he deals with. "We get the same material given to U.S. publications, without pertinent information like representatives in Canada and local prices. That means extra phone calls and wasted time."

He also is especially interested in articles with a Canadian perspective and says that unsolicited articles are almost never usable. "We need to talk to the Canadian user," he adds.

Both magazines are open to contact and visits from U.S. firms. "If you're making a tour, it's not much extra time or money to stop in Toronto and Montreal," says one.

One of the frustrations is that U.S. companies seem more aware of marketing, but don't devote resources to what is a significant market — Canada.

A final sobering thought: "The people I deal with do a pretty good job, the problem is all those I never hear from," says one editor.

Canada is too big a market to overlook — particularly when it's a country that is so interested in U.S. products and technology.

November 1986

TACTICS

Check Your Company's Pulse

"**Y**ou can't pick your route if you don't know your starting point." That's a truism in public relations. Equally true is its parallel quotation: "You can't pick your route if you don't know your destination." Careful research within and outside a company can help answer both of these very important issues.

The two elements of this research are traditionally called the "external audit" and the "internal audit." The names seem a bit pretentious; most "audits" I've seen have been superficial at best, enough to make a trained statistician chortle, much less the guy from the IRS who enthusiastically attacks your books with his portable computer. But even without statistical validity, this research can be extremely helpful. Nevertheless, it's amazingly rare, judging by the reactions to suggestions to conduct research from numerous clients and prospective clients and the results of those that we conduct.

Let's look at the reasons for conducting inside and outside audits and how to do them most efficiently.

One reason for this research is to determine the outside world's perceptions of a company and its products. That can help determine whether those perceptions are correct, desirable and widespread.

These are obviously extremely vital pieces of marketing information for anyone who is attempting to either reinforce or change a company's position in the minds of its key audiences.

Perhaps less obvious is the vital role that this research can play in answering other marketing questions for a company. These questions often extend far deeper than even choosing a desired position for a company in a particular market. Among the factors often clarified by such research are pricing points, unique sales features of the product, weakness of competitors, even the lack of a market for a product.

But the most important function of this research is to help answer the basic strategic questions facing a company: its strengths and weaknesses and opportunities and threats in the market.

Only by determining these factors can a firm choose a safe, or at least likely, strategy, including the position for the company that is most likely to be both credible and successful.

The critical questions in any research are what you're trying to find out and how you're going to conduct it.

Sometimes, it takes research - what you might call trial research - among a few of the key sources to help determine what questions should be asked. For a company already in a market, this kind of approach can be easier than for a firm that hasn't introduced itself or its products. In general, it's best to restrict the scope of the questions, since many of the important sources aren't very motivated to help out the company.

Who should do the research is another controversial question. There are many specialists, ranging from individuals to those prestigious and expensive management consulting firms that hire the cream of Harvard's MBA crop each year. Most larger companies have staff managers who specialize in this type ot research. A market research or advertising firm that specializes in consumer research is appropriate for large audiences.

Research can be done by phone, mail survey, in person, or some combination. Personal interviews are best in most respects but can obviously be very expensive and time consuming. Conversely, mailed surveys typically have low response: They're appropriate for large audiences but not as useful when you really want data from a certain select group of people. Phone interviews seem like the best compromise.

The usual people interviewed in an external audit are the press, important consultants and market analysts, Wall Street analysts, resellers, ultimate customers and, if possible, the competition.

Many of these people aren't very interested in helping, so it's critical to be concise; for some, it's best not even to say you're conducting a survey. It's better to simply sneak the questions into other conversations.

Reporters and editors in the general and business press, in particular, rarely want to help out in a survey. It's certainly not their job to help you, and most are very busy, so I don't blame them. Fortunately, if you have good relations with them, you can sometimes get the information you need. But don't abuse them or all of us will suffer in the future.

Internal audits, very important in helping understand your own firm, can be more extensive. The individuals interviewed are more motivated and probably willing to spend time giving detailed answers to many questions.

It's important to interview key managers separately to achieve the best results. Most are guarded in their answers if their bosses or peers are present. In most cases, the research should include top executives, plus representatives from all the important parts of the company, especially field sales and support people. It's often amazing how opinions differ about the company's strengths and weaknesses, its mission and its future direction.

Research into the perceptions about a company, both inside and outside the firm, is a vital part of determining the company's marketing plans, especially for communications and particularly for for public relations purposes. It needn't be a rigorous audit, but it's a necessary device too important to overlook.

September 1986

Orchestrate Product Introduction
for Maximum Impact

A product introduction is one of the more critical phases in the promotional cycle of a product. One of the better ways to optimize a firm's promotional resources is careful management of the time and effort involved in a major introduction; an almost obsessive attention to detail and schedules certainly helps.

Many elements need to be considered in achieving the most impact from a new product introduction, including planning: public relations, especially product publicity; collateral sales-support material; trade shows; space advertising; and internal notification of sales and other staff. But perhaps most important is coordination of these efforts. An absolute rule, as most marketers know, is no advertising before the publicity campaign is completed. And remember that the objective is to get maximum impact for an announcement. The objective is not to have a beautiful trade show exhibit, a lot of reporters at a press conference, or an ad appear in a specific issue of a magazine.

Promotion must be coordinated with product availability. This varies with the type of product and market. Ideally, consumer products should be available when promotion begins. The customer is excited; he or she should be able to buy the product immediately in a local store.

Once the ideal time for an announcement is decided, the planning begins. One problem that often occurs is the natural but unfortunate tendency to allocate time and energy to elements of the mix in proportion to their costs. Specifically, trade shows, slick collateral pieces, and advertising, which are relatively expensive, get a lot of attention. Public relations, internal notification, and less costly data sheets and application aids tend to get less attention. This can cause real problems and affect results.

Introducing products at trade shows is an old tradition for high-tech firms. Unfortunately, it's usually not a good idea if the definition of an introduction is the first public announcement. That first announcement should be made to your most important audiences, not just to people who happen to attend a trade show or conference.

In a concentrated and specialized market, a major announcement at a show can garner much attention and dominate a conference. But not at large, general shows like COMDEX, where even a big and well-known firm can get lost.

Although an exhibit at a large trade show helps reinforce your company's message, an exhibit on the floor isn't necessarily the best place to demonstrate your product. A private suite may be better, particularly if you can identify customers in advance or screen them at your booth.

Specialized conferences and publications are becoming more important forums for new product announcements. They offer a better way to achieve maximum editorial coverage with important audiences.

Maximizing editorial coverage is a whole subject in itself, but it certainly requires planning well in advance. It is possible to get extensive coverage in a number of publications almost simultaneously. Even multiple covers are a possibility, particularly for products with consumer appeal and visual interest like the Apple Macintosh or Hewlett-Packard Portable Computer.

Unfortunately, it's hard for a new company to get much

attention, so it's often a good idea to promote the firm first and introduce important products later.

Of course, when the product announcement is made — in any form — sales support literature is needed to respond to inquiries. Even a preliminary data sheet allows both the home office and field sales to respond. One good idea: a slick general sales piece containing less expensive inserts for specific products. This is particularly good for companies with many similar products.

The simplest but most important part of new product promotion is often overlooked: notifying people in the company about the new product. Timing is a critical issue here. Most firms are reasonably diligent about telling their own employees, but often neglect the important retailers, value-added resellers and independent representatives who face the customer. Proper notification can be tricky, since companies don't want to leak material prematurely; careful planning can let the word out without spilling the beans.

October 1984

Change Tactics to Meet Conditions

Computer and electronics technology advances with amazing speed, and the marketing of that computer and electronics technology must adapt almost as quickly.

This appears especially true in public relations. I've seen amazing changes in the success of public relations techniques over the past six years, based partly on the state of the market and partly on competition.

These changes are especially true for small, new companies. Big well-known firms with substantial resources have advantages in public relations, of course, though few use them.

IBM, in particular, can do whatever it wishes. If IBM wants to make an announcement, it does. And if that announcement is deemed important by the press, it takes priority over other news.

That's hardly surprising, or even unfair. IBM's $50 billion in computer sales dwarfs other computer and electronic firms, even the enormous but more diversified Japanese companies. And no matter what anyone says or wishes, IBM has incredible influence in setting standards and dominating the market. Even in areas where IBM has been a late entrant — personal computers, minicomputers and CAD — it has become the biggest player.

It's widely believed in the industry that Big Blue times announcements to hurt competitors as much as to help itself. All too frequently IBM has chosen to make an announcement at the last moment, completely destroying another company's carefully planned press conference or announcement.

So what can we do about IBM? In warfare, God is reputed to be on the side of the biggest battalions, but others, including startups like the original 13 colonies, often win enough battles to establish themselves.

These smaller organizations need two characteristics to succeed: intelligence and nimbleness. They have to be smart and fast. It's not easy to be smarter than IBM, but you can be swifter. And you can be smarter than a lot of the big organizations in the computer and electronics businesses without trying that hard.

What does this mean for public relations.

It means that we also have to move quickly. Look at the recent trends in public relations, for example. All have developed as smart but small companies have had to overcome the advantages of their big brethren.

Let's consider the classic way of introducing a major new product. It's the only method still acceptable to daily newspapers, broadcast and most news-oriented trade papers, by the way. The traditional product announcement was simple; a press release was sent simultaneously to all media, accompanied by a press conference for important products or big egos.

That worked fine once upon a time, but it didn't take long for clever companies to figure out a way to get additional publicity.

The traditional announcement was fine for big companies, since all relevant media reported what the big firms did even if some less timely magazines did it weeks later.

Unfortunately, this system had two major flaws: It reduced the news impact of the announcement, particularly in those vital magazines that have long lead times. Knowing that they'd be very late to publish the news they often played down the announcement.

Secondly, a company had little control over what happened to its announcement. This caused the development of the reverse announcement. We gave the longer-lead publications information in advance so they could publish the data at the same time as the more frequently published media (who hate this, of course). In exchange for this lead, the magazines could and did give better coverage of the announcement, even to the point of choosing exclusivity over importance. At an earlier time in the late '60's, we simply called up the appropriate reporters and editors long in advance and gave them the information they needed to write stories under a strict embargo.

This practice evolved into the organized press tour to visit editorial headquarters and try to convince editorial management to play the embargo game while giving the information to the reporter who would actually write the story.

Since publications have varying deadlines, this might necessitate more than one press tour, perhaps followed by a press conference at the end if the product and company were significant enough. One little problem was that by then, many of the media had the story, so they didn't want to attend a press conference, but we could sometimes overcome that with some new news.

An alternative that developed was to stage an event for customers, dealers and staff as the formal introduction rather than a true press conference. That made the introduction event news for the press, but only if the company or product justified it, as with the introduction of the Apple Macintosh or Compaq 386.

The flaw in all this is that any public relations person who's been around even for a short time knows the secrets, so magazine editors and reporters are getting tired of and resistant to press tours and personal visits, most of which aren't very productive.

As a result, I'm becoming convinced that we ought to reemphasize the earlier approach-planning carefully, then calling the appropriate reporters and editors and working around his or her schedule instead of just assuming a road tour or press conference is absolutely necessary. It may still require a trip to New York or Boston, but probably not to give the same product pitch to 20 editors who wish you'd just sent the information to the field reporter or market/product specialist in the first place. After all, few editorial managers write much and there are better uses for the time you spend with them.

December 1986

Make An Impact With Event Marketing

All of a sudden, "event marketing" is on everyone's lips. A term popularized by John Sculley, Apple's charismatic president, event marketing is an attempt to gain great media attention by staging an interesting, newsworthy event.

Apple has done it well. The company's events included annual meetings at which important product announcements were made with great fanfare, including extensive publicity in advance and elaborate presentations. Apple ran during the last two Super Bowls: the famous 1984 ad and the more recent "Lemmings."

. Apple isn't alone in its preoccupation with events. Lotus and Microsoft seem to be vying to stage the most elaborate and newsworthy parties, which have been widely discussed by an enthusiastic press. Seemingly, even computer nuts lust after the vicarious thrills we've come to associate more with Hollywood than with Silicon Valley.

Data General subscribed to the same theory for the introduction of its portable computer, orchestrating an impressive show at the Lincoln Center in New York.

Bruce & James, a tiny software publisher, did its own low-budget version of an event by inviting the press to lunch at McDonald's with the honest admission that they couldn't afford better, and publicized it as an event.

Of course, some industry reporters love this. At times, it

112

seems as if they envision themselves more as Rona Barrett or even *National Enquirer* sensationalists than as computer writers. There's no question that they're going for more splash than in the past.

This infatuation with event marketing may seem a bit of a turnaround in strategy for many marketers in the industry. For years, leading public relations experts counseled carefully planned leaks and interviews for the press in the belief that big press conferences result in less attention and less timely publicity.

Of course, there's not really any conflict between the two marketing approaches. These "events" aren't primarily for the press; they're for customers, dealers, stockholders, and analysts. The press focuses on the event, not the announcement. Naturally, however, product and other announcements usually receive significant publicity.

It should be noted that big shebangs don't work if they're just for the press. For one thing, the press is too jaded. They've seen too many other presentations. They usually won't show much enthusiasm, either – that's not their job. Most importantly, there aren't enough of them for the high level of energy needed for a big event.

Ironically, and not surprisingly, these events are a staple of the old-time publicist so scorned by the strategic-marketing-oriented public relations professional. These events sound suspiciously like elephants in the lobby at a bank opening or tightrope artists crossing between the towers of the World Trade Center.

On closer inspection, however, they're nothing but basic consumer publicity tools, and they can be very effective in getting attention - if done correctly.

The bottom line is: Do these events work? That is, do they garner publicity worth the usually substantial cost? More to the point, do they sell products?

The answer to the first question is yes. They can certainly generate publicity. Executed properly, they can even be very cost-effective. Unfortunately, event marketing works best for firms that are already well-known, a classic egg-and-chicken situation.

As for the second question, the jury remains out. The Lisa, introduced with great fanfare at elaborate events, wasn't successful. And Bruce and James has disappeared.

Whatever the value of this marketing strategy, others are jumping on the bandwagon. Expect to see more big events from computer companies. Just remember - they'd better be good if you expect them to have a significant impact in a highly competitive environment.

April 1985

Adapt Your Story to Your Audience

After 13 years of listening to company pitches as a member of the press and eight years preparing those company pitches as a public relations person inside and outside companies, I've come to some conclusions about the most effective way to present information.

Some of these ideas may have been influenced by the first job I had when I graduated from college — teaching algebra in a semi-rural, non-air-conditioned junior high school in southwest Florida. *The Washington Post* is more responsive to public relations pitches than those kids were to mathematics.

How to present information is very important to most of us because of the vital difference between sophisticated industrial and business marketing (which we do) and that of much truer consumer advertising and public relations. That differentiation is the educational content.

In industrial marketing, first we must learn, then we must teach. We learn from our clients, their customers, third parties and the competition. We teach the press, analysts and consultants, and they in turn teach their audiences. Often, we teach directly, through technical articles, seminars and collateral.

Most consumer promotion, by contrast, has little educational content, though companies like Mercedes Benz and Sharper Image have done a good job of appealing to our curious selves.

One problem with our audiences is their varying interests and knowledge. That's one reason I find the hierarchical approach the most effective way to reach them. The concept is simple: Develop a number of levels of messages. Present them sequentially until you've saturated the audience (it's easy to tell when you've reached that point—their eyes glaze over). The daily newspaper reporter is the first one you lose. Some super-techies and Wall Street types will follow you all the way to the end and then will ask for more.

In practice, the simplest message is a statement of the company's mission and position, all presented in one sentence. In effect, it's like the headline of a newspaper story. From that point, it progresses like a newspaper story — a short version, then a longer version and, finally, the version that's of interest only to those most interested, even committed.

The message must be conveyed on several tracks. Most reporters prefer a short release that focusses on the importance of the announcement plus longer background and detail material, rather than one long release. For trade reporters, detailed technical specifications are often preferred to wordy narratives that translate the same material into English that won't be used in their stories anyway.

Along with a hierarchical approach to developing messages, it's important to remember that different audiences respond best to different modes of presentation: written words, pictures and talking. This method is old stuff to any educator or psychologist, but critical if you want to get your message across.

Many people find that the easiest way for them to learn is by reading text, while some do better by seeing images and others by listening to someone explain things in words.

At the risk of oversimplifying — an unfortunate necessity in public relations — most engineers, scientists and artists prefer to be presented data in charts, graphs, tables and other pictures. I'm not sure if they enter those fields because of their inclinations, or if they're taught to understand relationships presented graphically, but it's true. And many of the reporters we deal with have a technical background, especially those writing for trade magazines.

On the other hand, most traditional writers are oriented toward words. But they fall into two categories, as do many other audiences: Some would rather hear the story (reporters), while others would rather read it (researchers).

You can see these contrasts in many instances: Some people like to listen to radio news and motivational cassettes. Others like to read books. Younger people tend to like fast-paced visuals — a preference learned from television, movies and MTV.

The result of these differences is that it's vital to present information in more than one form. That's why the combination of a traditional presentation, with slides which show relationships and comparisons, plus a good and interesting speaker talking, and the appropriate backup text, works so effectively.

Unfortunately, many people have trouble understanding how important other modes can be. Both as an editor and a public relations professional, I constantly harp about visual presentations because many of the people I've employed are word people. Quite a few of the charts and diagrams that clarify things for me (and many clients and editors) confuse them. We address this with seminars and individual coaching.

Sometimes, I suspect that we're dealing with differences so basic that there's no hope. But in less cynical moments, I'm convinced we can all learn other ways to communicate.

April 1986

Treat the Press Like Customers

At many computer companies, it's tough to get management committed to public relations. Particularly at older, more conservative firms, executives often regard public relations as someone else's job — specifically the job for public relations people.

These are the companies that don't get much press.

If you look at those companies that consistently get extensive and generally favorable coverage by the trade, consumer and business press, you'll find that their executives are very visible.

Conversely, those companies with little-known management tend to get little attention from the press.

In past years of searching for ways to convince managers to get more involved in both the planning and implementation of marketing-oriented public relations, I've finally discovered an approach that almost every executive understands. It's to treat the media and analysts as customers.

Any executive should understand the importance of customers, so this approach makes sense to most of them. If management doesn't consider customers important enough for their attention, I suspect that their companies aren't good places to work.

The beauty of regarding the press as customers is that it suggests parallels between the processes involved and the success rate.

Before we get too far into the analogy, however, let's look at how smart firms approach sales. The typical computer company uses a combination of direct and indirect sales, depending on the sales volume of the customer.

The smarter computer companies go further. They pick the largest and most strategic customers and elevate them to major account status. These few accounts — perhaps six to100, depending on the company's size — get assigned not only to specific sales personnel and sales management but also to company management.

The president may take a few of the top customers as his or her personal responsibility. This means that the president meets with top customers regularly, maintains phone contact and handles any major problems that arise.

It's an easy jump from this thinking to regarding the press and analysts as if they were customers.

A company typically has three groups of "gatekeepers." First are the key influencers. These are typically the dozen to 25 reporters, editors, and market analysts who make the biggest difference in your market. (A similar approach also works for investor, community and political relations, by the way.)

These people typically include a few editors from the key customer press (maybe at *Computerworld, PC Week* or *Electronic Engineering Times,* for example), key business and managememt press *(Business Week,* the local newspaper or *Electronic Business),* leading market watchers and analysts. The key contacts might be editorial management or they might be market specialists or the most relevant local reporters; each situation is different.

Some executives love dealing with the press, partly because this tends to stroke their egos and increases the chances for the personal visibility they deserve. Others will "adopt" editors only because they know it's important to the success of their firms. And a few executives simply won't cooperate. A few feel that It is beneath them, an ego problem that can hurt their companies.

When I was a reporter and editor, I know that I always responded when top executives took the time to meet with me, whether strictly in business or socially. Whether the executives were as uncommunicative as Ed de Castro of Data General or as ebullient as Jerry Sanders of Advanced Micro Devices' this contact often made the difference.

The executive who's willing to open his home or social life to the press almost always benefits in the long run, just as he would if he entertained the head of MIS for Metropolitan Life Insurance in similar ways. Few reporters from the business and trade press — there are exceptions — would shun or abuse this type of treatment.

The second tier of press and analysts includes all those important people who reach customers and prospects, but aren't quite as crucial. These people expect and deserve proper attention, too. In general, we find that assigning them to other company managers works well. These may be product or industry marketing managers, or engineering, research, financial or manufacturing management. This process ideally shouldn't go too low in the organization, and everyone who deals with the press must understand both the company strategy and limitations in disclosing information.

Realistically, company or agency public relations personnel usually have to remind or assign managers to talk to the press. This is typically when there is something significant to say, but if not, at least on a regular basis every few weeks.

In this way, the public relations professionals act as the sales force to the press, initiating contact that may need followup from others within the company. They also handle inquiries, take orders and close. Internal public relations people tend to react, whereas agencies often initiate programs and contacts.

Many computer companies sell through distribution as well as direct, of course. In a sense, that's analogous to the mailing of news releases and distribution over news wires and other indirect means. This is an effective means of reaching the less vital press, who could still be very important.

Some public relations professionals, and most members of the press, might find this approach to dealing with the media offensive. But those who've been in sales know its value.

This approach also helps promote public relations internally. I know it's won over some of our recalcitrant clients, and it might work for your executives, too.

February 1988

Use Public Relations for
1½- Way Communications

Everyone who reads this publication knows the value of public relations in communicating with any company's target audiences: the press, analysts, consultants, resellers, employees, government and the community, prospects and customers. But not everyone is aware of public relations' function as a means for those audiences to communicate back to the company.

The return communication is perhaps not as strong as the primary one; that's why I call public relations a 1½-way communications medium, not a two-way channel.

One major function of public relations in most organizations is conducting research, gathering and analyzing data that helps a company understand the attitudes and perceptions of its chosen audiences. This is clearly a type of communications, one that is not restricted to public relations, but to any operation that performs or manages research.

The interviews used in research can often return significant information beyond that requested. This is especially true in questioning customers and resellers. It's highly desirable to perform at least some of these interviews in person, which allows the respondent to comment on many subjects beyond those under immediate inquiry. For that reason, interviewers should be encouraged to dig deep and report on any peripheral comments, not just those specified. This generally requires an interviewer familiar with the company and its markets.

But formal research projects only provide one form of feedback from second and third parties. Some of the most significant is informal, and many company officials, and even public relations professionals, don't appreciate its importance.

Quite bluntly, information can be collected informally from reporters and analysts. This can be tricky. Many reporters consider it unethical or short-sighted to share information that they haven't published, and when they've received information under embargo, that's certainly true. But many are willing to talk, especially if they like you and are sure they won't get in trouble.

In general, the reporters who are most likely to be very useful are experienced trade magazine editors and reporters. They're often very knowledgeable and feel close to the people and companies they work with, even competent and empathetic public relations personnel. There's a misconception that people fawn over reporters, but that's not true for the majority of reporters and editors in the trades. Most know a great deal, have strong opinions, and love to talk on the rare occasion that anyone asks them what they think.

It's not just a matter of calling one of them up when you need information however. In most cases, you need to develop an ongoing relationship with the reporter.

The best way to get to know a reporter is generally the most obvious. Get together often, talk on the phone and provide useful information, including material and ideas that aren't self-serving. Effective public relations people don't wait until they need a reporter, but call and meet in advance.

There are many other ways to meet informally with journalists: Invite them to your firm or to the clients' firm, whether to meet with executives or simply to talk about the companies. Invite them to your agency, to address the staff and help everyone save time by focusing on what the reporter wants and needs. Attend professional meetings and promotional events when editors visit or speak. Write personal letters, which many reporters say are becoming rare. Drop by their offices occasionally if they welcome it, perhaps bringing some information they might need. Call and schmooze, if they're open to this — some aren't.

All these contacts give you a chance to find out what their magazines are doing and often provide an excellent chance to learn what your competitors are also doing.

It's not just public relations people who can be good spies. Almost any time corporate executives meet with a reporter, they learn important information. They're not likely to learn as much as they tell, but that's why this is a $1\frac{1}{2}$- way channel, not two-way.

A good idea, though difficult to achieve, is for the public relations person as well as executives to schedule regular meetings with the key editors. A competent secretary or tickler system is the key, I suppose, but it sure helps to have enough time as well!

One other idea: Since most reporters call major companies they follow on a regular basis, it would be useful for the companies to reciprocate, as long as they have some useful information for the reporter.

You'll note that my comments have focused on trade magazine editors and reporters. For various reasons, the comments don't apply to trade newspapers, or general or business magazines or newspapers.

Most newspaper reporters identify more with their readers than their sources, so they aren't as likely to consider helping you as important or even proper. Most of these other reporters aren't as close to the details as trade magazine editors, either. They tend to have shorter assignments, less industry and technical knowledge and more independence as well.

Analysts and consultants are another matter. Many charge for their opinions (which may be worth something). They tend to believe they should be paid when you want something from them. If they're not clients, they still might be pleasant people, might want to assist potential clients, or get visibility for themselves, however. It all depends on the individual.

In summary, reporters and analysts can provide much information to help us in planning or implementing marketing and public relations programs. Public relations isn't just a broadcast medium; it can provide receiver feedback as well.

April 1987

Defuse Marketing Crises

D ealing with marketing crises is a standard part of the traditional public relations curriculum, but such crises are usually toxic leaks, accidents or other community problems. Sometimes crises are financial: losses, layoffs, government investigations and, more and more common in the computer business, bankruptcies.

Some of these problems could be considered marketing crises - a bankruptcy concerns customers, distributors and retailers who don't want to be stuck with orphan equipment.

But there are other crises in marketing that also need careful public relations attention. Second only to Chapter 11, so it seems, is IBM entering a company's market. Perhaps as serious is IBM introducing a new product into a market it's already serving, IBM slashing prices or IBM abandoning a market. In fact, the discontinuance of the PCjr and its subsequent dumping seems to have dealt the home-computer market a staggering blow. After all, if IBM, with all of its resources can't make it in a market, who can?

What are some other marketing crises? Competitors cutting prices or introducing far superior products. Respected marketing managers jumping ship in midstream and joining a competitor. Salespeople bailing out en masse. Distributors resigning. Advertising campaigns bombing. Products late. Products that don't work. Lawsuits.

In many of these cases, public relations can help the

situation. But it can rarely fix it. If products don't work, only the engineers can solve the real problem, not public relations people. Public relations, however, offers many tools that can help minimize problems. Unfortunately, many of these steps have to be taken in advance, before a crisis hits.

It should be obvious that every company should develop contingency plans in advance. But it's rarely done, both because of the optimism of most high-tech marketers and because of the pressures of today's business. And no matter how carefully a company may plan, problems may arise from unexpected sources.

Nevertheless, a few basic questions should be addressed in preparation for any emergency. Does your company have good press contacts? Do you know who you would appoint for your spokesperson in the event of a crisis? Is your agency or staff prepared to respond to a situation at a moment's notice?

Sometimes, a manager or public relations person with extensive experience, fast reactions and good judgment is worth far more than detailed planning.

Whatever the prior planning for emergencies, the prime rule of managing a marketing crisis is to develop relationships with key press contacts in advance. Good reporters wouldn't kill an important story just because they know you or even because they're close friends of yours. But they're almost certain to try to get your side of the question and perhaps even consider your firm's viewpoint if they know you as a person.

Just as important is having a spokesperson available to the press. "No comment" and "The firm didn't return phone calls by publication time" seem to be admissions of guilt, no matter what justification is given.

On the other hand, few people within a company should be allowed to talk to the press, even if it means warning all employees to refer calls to certain spokespersons. And those people should be confident, knowledgeable and credible.

A top executive is usually the best spokesperson from a public relations standpoint, but that executive should be well prepared, known to the press and skilled in media relations. Lawyers are usually the worst spokespeople (unless they just happen to have a law degree but serve another function in the company). A high-level public relations professional is often used, but the president, chairman of the board or CEO is more credible, and most journalists prefer quoting from the top.

Whoever is chosen should be an employee of the company. An employee from an external agency, such as a lawyer or even an outside public relations agency, appears somewhat suspect, as if the company has something to hide.

A written statement should be prepared and distributed to those who may be dealing with the press in an emergency. This helps ensure consistency, but that statement should not be read in an obvious way to the press. Paraphrasing by a competent spokesperson is preferable unless the subject is so sensitive that the lawyers overrule good press-relations practice.

Finally, honesty is the best long-term policy. You should be as open as is practical. If you aren't honest, the firm will live to regret it in the future. On the other hand, there's no need to volunteer information, especially negative information, unless it's vital or relevant (which may be determined by the lawyers, particularly when it concerns a public company).

And remember that even the most credible company or spokesperson has only so many silver bullets. Don't use them frivolously or capriciously. You just may need them in the future.

November 1985

Measure Public Relations Success

Trying to measure public relations effectiveness drives consumer-trained advertising people nuts. Clients or prospective clients well versed in the sophisticated techniques that are used to evaluate mass product advertising invariably throw up their hands in bewilderment after grilling public relations people mercilessly on justifying their work.

For that reason, I've spent a lot of time thinking about the best ways to judge public relations efforts. It's rarely a matter of evaluating whether these efforts are effective at all because most marketers realize that public relations is cost effective compared to most other marketing programs. The questions usually are *how* effective and what types of objectives are to be accomplished.

But before getting into some of the approaches to measurement, let's look at why public relations is hard to evaluate.

Public relations rarely is the only tool used to publicize products or influence perceptions about a company. Advertising, direct mail, company literature, sales representatives and even the company's past reputation may have a significant impact on customers.

In addition, most public relations activities are aimed at intermediaries, not end users. Public relations seeks to influence influencers: the media, analysts, consultants. They in turn spread the word. To judge public relations results fairly, then, you need to find how the program is influencing these intermediaries. Pre- and post-surveys sound perfect.

But most of these people don't like to be polled. Aside from newcomers or cooperative trade-press editors, the media generally considers being surveyed a nuisance at best. Daily papers, consumer and general-business press and broadcast media are sometimes downright offended (and offensive) when approached. Their attitude is "We don't work for you or your clients. We work for our readers. Don't bother us."

Given this situation, try to minimize the number of surveys and make them as painless as possible. A few short questions are the limit; even better is sending out a blind questionnaire.

Aside from problems of surveying the media and analysts, however, other measures are available: counting inches or articles, tabulating sales leads, listing subjective impressions and evaluating coverage against outlined objectives.

Let's start with counting inches or articles. This is the first inclination of most public relations beginners. A few public relations agencies guarantee results or charge by the published piece, but they are considered pariahs by traditional public relations people, like physicians who charge only if they cure an illness.

The problem with counting inches or articles is two-fold: It's easier to get into some publications than others, and quantity isn't always a measure of quality. It's my experience that a sentence in The Wall Street Journal may be worth pages in a minor publication or even a major trade magazine.

Public relations people, no matter how effective, ultimately can't control their audiences. Sometimes, even comparing results in the press to those of competitors is tough, since a well-known person or well-established company tends to get more media attention.

Counting sales leads isn't a very good way to measure public relations results, either. In fact, that's not really public relations' forte (see next page). You can do it, but public relations is better for influencing than action.

Subjective attitudes aren't really measures, but they can give a useful indication of changes in perception. One of our clients once mentioned that he had noticed a major change during the year that we had been working together, not just with the media and customers but with competitors (many of whom were old friends), now taking him more seriously as a force in the market.

And now the best way to evaluate public relations: evaluating coverage against established goals. Every public relations program should have a written plan, with specific relevant and realistic objectives. These objectives could include items as simple as being mentioned in target publications on a periodic basis to something as complex as being recognized as a market leader by 80 percent of the 20 leading influence makers (intermediaries) in a given industry segment.

The first accomplishment is easy to measure. But the second requires a more sophisticated analysis of the content of coverage received in important publications or from specific individuals.

Content analysis involves looking at all of your media coverage over a specified period of time and identifying which articles, research reports or broadcast clips support or detract from public relations objectives. The results can be reported quantitatively, providing an indication or not just how often you were able to gain attention but how effective you were at communicating specific messages.

Content analysis can be done formally — there are several firms that specialize in offering this service — or informally by your own staff or agency.

But in setting public relations goals and establishing a program to analyze news coverage against goals, don't forget that you and your agency can't accomplish much without cooperation from others on your staff. Few things are more frustrating than calling *Fortune* or *Business Week* to call off interviews because a chief executive balks at the last moment, changing his mind about an agreed-upon objective.

Based on January 1986 column

Generate Inquiries
with Public Relations

Most marketers rarely think about it, but public relations is not usually the best way to generate sales leads. Though we've all heard the stories about piles of bingo cards resulting from the occasional article or product announcement, that's the exception.

Instead, public relations is better for influencing people, changing their perceptions about a company, educating them about the uses for a product, increasing credibility, announcing new products, or generating favorable reviews. But with a little thought, public relations can also help generate sales leads.

It's important to remember that other promotional techniques are superior to publicity for generating leads. Advertising is generally better; it offers more control such as listing toll-free telephone numbers or bingo numbers (in some publications), including coupons or reply cards. Above all, direct mail excels at reaching qualified leads, as is evident every time I open my mail. Direct response advertisers have learned the psychology of respondents, with Publishers Clearing House perhaps the best example in this field.

But back to getting names via public relations. First, choosing media is critical. Some publications and broadcast in general are notoriously poor choices. The daily paper doesn't list phone numbers or addresses in news stories, for example. And it provides no means of reader response such as bingo cards.

Publications such as *Electronic News* and *Business Week* fit into the same class. It takes a highly motivated reader to respond to an announcement in one of these publications. On the other hand, they're great for getting the word out and influencing opinion, not always positively, as we all know.

Conversely, some publications are great for getting piles of mail. This is especially true of hobbyist publications. A bingo in a true hobbyist magazine will fill up the company's mail box, but the company may not want the names unless they're distributing mail-order catalogues.

A quasi-hobbyist magazine like *Byte* or *InfoWorld* is also a great lead generator, but it's up to the company to qualify the respondents. I'll warn you, though, that the phone calls and letters can drive marketing and sales staff nuts. Hundreds of unqualified replies aren't unusual.

The secret to getting good qualified leads is to start with the media that has the right end audience — but remember that those most popular with management aren't likely to be good for generating names. Executives don't fill out bingo cards or respond directly. Instead, they pass notes along to subordinates. And those subordinates are more likely to call the local sales rep than fill out a card to get information.

Among the best media for generating leads are those read by real engineers. They love to collect data, much of which they read and consult. *Electronic Engineering Times,* for example, is a great place for bingo leads; the newspaper format seems ideal for this application. Other engineering magazines are also good, though as hinted before, the higher the position of the readership, the poorer the direct response may be. In particular, *Electronic Products,* with a widely dispersed readership at many smaller companies, usually does better than *Electronic Design,* which is more concentrated at bigger companies and includes many engineering managers among its readership. Once the media is understood, it's necessary to look at the specific form of editorial that generates leads. Highest quality usually comes from bingos associated with technical feature articles. A reader usually is fairly interested if he or she gets to the end of the article and indicates an interest in obtaining more information. Bingos associated with news items are also the source of good leads, though few publications include them. Surveys are also good sources, particularly when the reader can pick out specific products from a company rather than just give a general indication of interest.

The best bingo responses are to new-product features and new-product listings. These can be useful, and it's very easy for the reader to check off several items without much thought.

One of the biggest lead generators is substantial-looking literature such as data books or extended application materials. Likewise, free product samples and design helps seem to excite even the most somber and staid engineering managers. I'd hesitate to offer these items through public relations; it's too hard to control them.

That brings up the question, "What do you do with these leads?" Something intelligent, I hope. There's a story circulating, for example, that a major semiconductor company threw away thousands of names from well-controlled publications each month because it only wanted to respond to leads from its own advertising supplement. It's silly to waste leads; better not to get them than to ignore them.

The most obvious use for leads is to send them to the local sales office, distributor or dealer, but experience has proven that most of these people ignore the leads unless they know the names or are forced to call them by sales management.

Public relations can generate sales leads. It's up to the company whether it wants these leads and whether it uses them effectively once it has them.   *October 1985*

Budget for Public Relations

The first question a smart company asks about public relations is, "Who should do it?" The second question that company should be asking is, "How much should we budget for public relations?"

There's no easy answer to the second question. It's entirely dependent on the market you want to reach, the impact you want to make and the time frame you have chosen. A big impact on a broad market in a short period of time means it's necessary to spend more money for public relations. Conversely, given proper lead time for preparation, narrow markets can be reached efficiently and effectively with less money.

Let's look at some specifics, complete with some necessary over-simplifications.

If you look at the major groups of buyers you need to reach, they fall into interesting multiples of 10 (orders of magnitude, if you wish).

By looking at these audiences, you can estimate how much money it will cost to reach them. Before a company is ready to appear in public, only a small group of key influencers, namely a few press people and some market experts, need to be reached. Later, the list will expand, but that doesn't imply a direct relation to cost. It obviously costs less per person to reach a large group. But it's more expensive to market a consumer product than one aimed at a small select group such as design engineers.

IMPORTANT MARKET-BUYING SEGMENTS

AUDIENCE	APPROXIMATE SIZE
Key influencers	10
Relevant press	100
OEMs	1,000
Dealers/VARS or Fortune 1000 executives	10,000
Design engineer/DP managers	100,000
Active investers or DP Professionals	1 million
Small businesses or managers and professionals	10 million
True consumers	100 million

Another consideration is the impact you want to make or need to make, for that matter. Studies by the Strategic Planning Institute show that the market leader gets most of the profits, while second- and third-place firms end up splitting a smaller slice. The rest share crumbs - if there are any left.

I've noticed that it takes a certain level of effort — and spending — to make any difference with public relations or advertising. Spend less than that level and you're wasting money; spend more and you're wasting money. Between these limits, however, the rule is: the more you spend, the more effective you can be.

Unfortunately, I can't give much guidance on actual dollar amounts or useful measurement of impact. It can be done in one specific market segment, but only after extensive study and experience. It is possible to make a big impact on a small market, like test and measurement, for $50,000 to $100,000 per year, for example. But to effectively reach all owners of small businesses would cost at least three or four times as much.

It's also fallacious to think that you can set budgets as a percentage of sales. That may be relevant for a stable product but not when you're trying to gain market share or create a new market for a product. And some markets require heavier spending than others. Some cosmetics firms spend 50 percent of revenues on advertising for some product lines, and the same is often true for new products aimed at a broad market, especially software.

PERCENTAGE OF BUDGET ALLOCATIONS

(Companies with sales of more than $100 million)

	Marketing	Advertising	Public Relations
Large supplier, stable market	5	1	0.1
Dynamic firm or market	10	5	0.5
Dynamic firm and market	20	10	2.0

Just as an exercise for fun, however, I've included a comparison of typical expenditures in percentages by companies with sales of more than $10 million.

The last factor to affect cost is timing. It clearly costs more to do things fast and still make an impact. Six or nine months is generally needed to plan and execute an important new-product introduction.

In practice, that rarely happens in our business. So a public relations program ends up costing more and isn't as effective as it could be with more time to plan and execute.

In particular, there are limited opportunities for some types of public relations if you have insufficient time. Newspapers with fast turnaround aren't usually the best place for product introductions, for example. Slick magazines are, but in most cases, they take months of lead time.

February 1986

Coordinate Advertising And Public Relations

Everyone involved in advertising and public relations agrees that the two complementary disciples should work together. But few do it. Advertising and public relations can work together, and it's really not that difficult.

Cooperation benefits all those involved in the process, including those working in advertising, public relations, and, not surprisingly, the targets of this cooperation: the client or the employer.

Certainly, anyone in marketing should know the first rule about public relations and advertising: Don't ever advertise a new product before its publicity campaign is underway.

Ideally, all critical publicity should appear before an ad program starts because many publications regard any product that has been advertised as old news and, as a result, will not cover it or will reduce coverage dramatically.

The only exceptions would be a product so important or a campaign so noteworthy that publications can't ignore them or treat them as news. Two examples would be the introductions of the Apple Macintosh and the "new" Coke.

Realistically, some publications pay more attention to these issues than others. Also, ads on introduction day (the day a press conference occurs or the first major publicity hits) in publications read by the media such as *The New York Times* and the *Wall Street Journal* can increase coverage in weekly trade publications the next Monday, but it's tricky.

This technique would be true primarily for a less exciting product in which an extensive marketing campaign might be a signal to the press that the product is important.

Having disposed of the most pressing questions, let's take a look at more fundamental considerations of cooperation between the disciplines of advertising and public relations.

The first consideration is organization. Companies have many ways to handle marketing communications, from an internal organization that does it all to almost complete dependence on outside agencies without even an internal communications specialist.

Having one person supervising both the advertising and marketing public-relations functions can simplify things in a company, although I believe it's important to have strong advocates for each discipline. Except in the smallest company, it's difficult for a single person or group to do both well since they require such different talents.

In many cases, the top marcom person is an advertising specialist by background, so it's important to have a strong public relations person involved to maintain balance. In other cases, a public-relations person is the supervisor, so a good ad or sales-promotion specialist provides balance.

Whatever the organization, it's important that basic strategy and plans be presented to all of those involved simultaneously. Likewise, the advertising and public-relations groups should share their ideas and programs.

Sometimes, the advertising and public relations people feel competitive, whether in trying to be the star or seeking budgets or getting their programs accepted by the client. Advertising and public-relations counterparts should occasionally meet the client separately to help restore sanity.

In developing plans, it's important to remember what advertising and public relations do best: Public relations is great for handling product introductions, for example, while advertising is better for following up and continuing the reinforcement needed after the first burst of publicity on a new product. Likewise, advertising is better for promoting brand names, while the press is notoriously independent in such matters. Advertising is great for a concentrated message geared to a restricted audience, while public relations is good for reaching broader audiences at lower cost.

All these examples mean that it's easy to design a program that utilizes each discipline to its fullest. Use public relations for the introduction and use advertising afterwards.

The synergy between public relations and advertising can be accomplished only by a great deal of careful planning and a certain amount of subjugation to the common good. It's great for an advertising agency to be producing and running those television spots or ads in *The Wall Street Journal*, for example, but wouldn't it be better for the company if the advertising were concentrated on more dedicated markets such as retailers or committed computer advocates.

July 1986

Use Newswires For Maximum Impact

For decades, public relations professionals have focused on one method of news dissemination: the mailed news release. Other techniques have been used, but generally only by exception. If the news were really hot and important, or had to be disclosed promptly by law, it went out over a paid news wire. And then we could only hope that the news made it into the United Press International, Associated Press or Dow Jones circuit.

I think it's time to rethink our basic attitudes about news release distribution. I base that opinion on several facts:

• Paid news wire transmission of information is now probably cheaper than maintaining mailing lists, printing and postage.

• Most media can now accept computer data directly.

• Publications receive so much mail that many reporters discard everything but individually addressed envelopes.

I'm convinced that newswires such as BusinessWire and PR Newswire are now the primary transmission methods required for most news stories.

We still need to use the mail, however, for items with photographs, such as new product stories, and releases for publications serving narrow niches. In these cases, it's worthwhile to mail the material separately since newswire transmission of photos isn't generally practical for most applications yet. Also, many trade and other magazines don't get newswires directly, although BusinessWire goes to about 75 computer and electronic trade and special-interest publications. This includes weekly trade newspapers.

Some other publications get the releases from public databases such as Dialog and CompuServe.

It has taken me a while to accept this idea. Part of the reason I've resisted abandoning old ideas was that when I was a reporter, we didn't have the same type of services. Some are very new.

At McGraw-Hill in Los Angeles, in the early '70s when I worked for *Electronics*, we received hot news over a cranky and slow teleprinter from one service. We dutifully opened all the mail. Few things came by wire.

It's different now. A number of newspaper and magazine reporters have told me that they throw away all their computer-addressed mail. But they look at copy from news wires, either in printed form or on their computer screen, since many publications receive the wire directly.

News wires have been steadily increasing their coverage, too. They can reach most major international audiences.

Again, using BusinessWire as an example, one of their packages of outlets reaches more than 90 Japanese computer and electronics publications, a hard group to address, and the cost is reasonable. Similar deals also apply in Europe.

These newswire services have developed a number of specialized packages in the United States, too, including a news wire service that specializes in sports news. This is a hot new subject that has some relevance for high-technology promotion.

I mentioned before that newswires aren't the ideal method of sending photos yet, but they're trying to get there. BusinessWire has been mailing sheets with lots of little photos out to the press since mid-1986. Then, if editors are interested, they can order full-size versions. Again, they get them by mail. This is a useful service, but one already available from other sources. And it's for features, not breaking news developments.

But true satellite distribution of photos is about to begin. It will take eight minutes to transmit a black-and-white photo, half an hour for color (with the separations).

With all these new developments in paid wire services, however, the most interesting may be direct access to the financial community.

In the past, we could transmit material required of publicly-held companies for financial disclosure over a wire, hoping that Dow Jones would pick it up and transmit it to analysts and brokers.

Dow Jones often did, but in condensed form. And they have certain restrictions, such as company size, that keep them from distributing material important to many companies.

The public relations wire services were required to delay their transmissions 15 minutes behind actual media delivery.

Perhaps more interesting, Bridge Information Services, a database widely used by analysts and brokers, is now providing the full text of all financial releases that go over the BusinessWire. That means that this is now a medium of disclosure, not just a means to get to the medium of disclosure (such as Dow Jones).

These recent developments underscore the rapid changes that keep us hopping in public relations. The next step, I suppose, will be when we can directly address individual customers. It's possible now via CompuServe, but appears a long way from widespread application.

February 1987

Market by Subpoena

Suddenly, everyone is suing everyone. Apple is suing Microsoft and Hewlett-Packard. Lotus is suing Paperback Software; Intel is suing NEC; AMD is suing everyone. What happened to our chummy world of high technology? Why this sudden rash of lawsuits?

Have lawyers replaced engineers and marketers as the corporate heroes? High-technology companies have always prided themselves on their abilities to compete on the basis of innovation, nimbleness, process expertise and even marketing. Now they've decided that lawsuits are a preferred means of competition.

Some of the actions are downright funny:

• Apple, which "borrowed" user interface imagery from Xerox for its Macintosh, is suing Microsoft and Hewlett-Packard for what it claims are products too similar to its own.

• Advanced Micro Devices, which started in business by "second sourcing" other companies' products, is now suing others for what it claims is patent infringement.

• Lotus, whose 1-2-3 looks an awful lot like the VisiCalc and SuperCalc I once used, is suing Adam Osborne's Paperback Software for copying Lotus' "look and feel."

Most of the suits are less ironic, but all have serious implications for the plaintiff, the defendants and our indus-

145

try. And many of those implications involve marketing and public relations issues.

It's clear that these companies have every right to sue anyone they think is appropriating their ideas unfairly, but the way many of them are pursuing the suits indicates that they're more interested in the marketing and public relations value of these suits than in sincerely trying to redress wrongs.

In the first place, many of the companies sued have been in serious negotiations for patent licenses or other arrangements.

Perhaps more significantly, most of the companies sued have learned about the suits when reporters called them to solicit their comments. When you're serious about a suit, you serve notice first. You don't issue a press release.

The real reasons for many of these suits are to gain favorable publicity, to scare potential customers of the firm sued or to try to gain a favorable position in negotiations for royalties, licenses or other considerations.

Let's look at each possible reason: A company that sues firms for patent infringement or other reasons is asserting its leadership. No one copies followers. Gaining publicity from an announcement of a suit helps a firm that wants to be perceived as an innovator and casts doubt on the copier in this technology/innovation-oriented world.

Perhaps more significantly, the suits represent a means to cast doubt on the ability of the defendant to deliver the product in question or even to continue to exist.

In truth, most of these suits are settled, and the products continue to be sold (sometimes with changes), and the company sued continues to exist. But the whole process certainly casts a pall over the sued firm and its products. We only need look at the people who bought Kodak instant cameras, then couldn't buy film for them after Polaroid won its suit (even though some of Kodak's film was superior!)

And of course, most of the suits are settled, but the plaintiff wants to get the best deal it can, either royalties or cross-licensing in most cases.

But what do you do if you're sued?

The first step is to talk to your lawyer — and your public relations counsel. If, as is common, the first word of the suit is from a reporter, you can understand the motivation for the suit.

It's wise not to make any substantial response until you've seen the legal filing. Based on that, give a straightforward response. In 90% of the cases, it's "We have investigated the situation carefully and do not believe that the suit has any merit."

It's worth expanding on the issues, of course, and it's especially important to prepare your own staff. Tell them not to talk to the press, leaving that to a few executives qualified to speak. Even for them, prepare specific questions and answers.

It's vital to respond as quickly as possible, since clever companies time these actions to make it difficult for those sued to get a fair shake with the press. The announcements often come just before publication deadlines, so it's hard for the company under fire to respond. And it's undesirable to be quoted with a "No comment," which always implies guilt to most observers.

I'm not a lawyer, but I suspect that you might also want to countersue, especially if it looks like the suit might affect your business. And in most cases I've worked on, it has.

Of course, there is the other side of the issue. There can be a lot of public relations value in bringing a suit. As I mentioned, even omitting the many justified and legitimate legal actions that occur, suing someone can be a good marketing strategy.

Such an action can backfire, however. The press can cast

your firm as a nasty Goliath oppressing a small David. And though that was hardly the case with Apple versus Hewlett-Packard and Microsoft, the press in general was very negative toward Apples' action. Apple, which had carefully nurtured the image of a counterculture free spirit, was suddenly clearly in the role of a big, litigious firm — and those companies are usually seen as rigid and lacking in innovation.

No one had the same attitude toward Adam Osborne's company, of course, since he had developed an unfavorable reputation as an arrogant know-it-all among the press. But Lotus doesn't enjoy a great reputation for its press relations, either.

My biggest concern about these suits, however, is that some companies with reputations as leaders now seem to be changing their strategy to building walls and digging moats rather than attacking. This whole trend seems a sign of decline, one that I would not associate with the industry I serve.

October 1988

Approach Broadcast Media
For Additional Publicity

H igh-tech companies tend to think of public relations opportunities in terms of print media — and for good reason. Magazines and newspapers are well-known and understood, whereas broadcasting can seem mysterious, confusing, and even intimidating.

It's also difficult to judge the value of broadcast exposure. There's little question that seeing your product or company president on TV is exciting. But what is the real benefit beyond that? Does it sell products or stocks? How many people actually see it?

Broadcast exposure, though ephemeral, appears to be gaining in importance every day. It will become vital when the present MTV and video-game generation becomes serious buyers of high-technology products, since they are so oriented toward broadcast.

The most obvious way to get into broadcast is through advertising. It's essential for many consumer high-tech products and has suddenly become chic, even for business-oriented software packages. A number of firms — notably Lotus and Ashton-Tate — have spent vast amounts of money on mass TV advertising. However, it may not be a good use of resources. Symphony and Framework may be excellent products, but it's not likely they'll be sold to enough people to justify the high costs of network TV exposure.

Many high-tech products are too narrow for broadcast

advertising, but may be great for more limited audiences, including cable, public, educational, and other specialized programming.

As with print media, broadcast offers many opportunities for editorial or nonpaid exposure: news/magazine shows, talk shows, as well as science, educational, and technology programs. Some are easier to penetrate than others, but in all cases, opportunities and actual exposure are limited. For those accustomed to print, TV is fleeting. A few seconds of exposure is typical, and a minute is rare on major programs.

The three forms of broadcast available are radio, local and national TV, and specialized cable.

Major opportunities in radio are hot news and talk shows and sometimes live call-ins.

As one might imagine, it's easier to get on local TV than national TV. Most local stations are interested in newsworthy events involving local firms. To find the proper contact, get in touch with the general news-assignment editor, then ask who covers the business and technology areas.

While it's not easy to get on national TV, many programs and spots that originate locally are distributed nationally; others originate from specific network operations in major broadcast centers. It can be confusing, so be persistent.

As with radio and daily newspapers, late-breaking news can completely blow a story, even when strong interest has been indicated. One of the classic cases was Advanced Micro Devices' newsworthy award of a million dollars to a production-line worker. All the right TV people were there when the worker was told about the award one Sunday morning. But later that day, the Iranians took the U.S. embassy hostage and most of the AMD publicity was killed.

Cable TV, and perhaps new, low-power broad stations, hold the strongest potential for effective publicity for high-tech companies. Narrow-casting is the visual equivalent of the highly segmented magazine and newspaper business. Unfortunately, it's only recently become a reality.

One of the most obvious opportunities for broadcast publicity is daily news programs; they're a popular format for most stations, and a great place to gain visibility.

Most news coverage, not surprisingly, is based on events: a news conference introducing a product, a visit from a vice-presidential candidate, even a crisis such as a toxic spill or fire. While pivotal products such as the Macintosh and Hewlett-Packard's Portable Computer have received quite a bit of coverage, a product without much consumer appeal is hard to get on the news. Therefore, to get TV news coverage, it's almost vital to stage an event.

Visuals make television more interesting. Showing an unusual product or process with something moving is more effective than people talking. Conversely, radio news is often in interview form. For radio, interesting sounds such as synthesized voices will garner more attention.

Magazine programs and talk shows are two types of programming where producers are likely to respond to pitches with less of a news peg.

The magazine format usually allows up to 10 minutes of time, enough to develop a story. Like a magazine, however, it often requires a surprisingly long time to pitch, produce, and appear. Six months from initial proposal to appearance isn't unusual. For most of these programs, human interest is the key.

Talk shows are more topical. They require little preparation, so they can air quickly. They do demand an interesting subject and often include a product demonstration, but to be successful they need an excellent source. Unfortunately, many high-tech excutives don't make the best interviews: They may be nervous, or unable to give lucid, articulate, concise — even glib — answers to questions. The worst interviewees for TV are people who give either a one-word or 20-minute response.

Two other good opportunities are the growing number of computer, science, and technology-oriented shows. It seems there's a new one every week, including a whole cable network, and some interesting new forms of narrowcasting that reach specific audiences. These programs include Nova on PBS.

In general, these specialized shows may be more accessible, especially if they are local, but impact is difficult to judge. In some cases, the time and money committed appear disproportionate to the return. One of the best uses for these programs, in fact, may be tapes shown for employee morale and for sales purposes at conventions and seminars.

Some excellent opportunities exist on general-business and investment-oriented shows buried within general-news networks or programs. Many of these programs have large, and more significantly, quality audiences.

And don't forget truly educational programs aimed at both children and adults. These provide excellent opportunities, sometimes with minimal effort and expense.

One often overlooked method of getting TV exposure is placing products on visible programs. Specialists at placing products charge $25,000 a year and up, but sometimes it can be arranged through other contacts. Producers are becoming more sophisticated, and often charge for this service.

The biggest problem with broadcast is its fleeting nature. If you miss it, it's gone. However, simple techniques like repetition of programs, as well as sophisticated selective distribution and storage mechanisms, are making broadcast an even more attractive public-relations vehicle.

November 1984

Try Top-Down Public Relations

Most people have a natural tendency to do what's easy for them. For public relations practitioners marketing computer products, that often translates to taking the same approach with the same publications — and consequently getting the same type of coverage.

I'd like to suggest another approach, one I call *top-down public relations*. The concept is simple: always shoot for the biggest hits you can, then work down from there.

This may sound obvious, but it's the opposite of the way many public relations people operate. In practice, top-down public relations translates to a whole new way of thinking, one that generally aids in getting better publicity even in publications you normally approach.

This doesn't mean traditional coverage isn't important. The media read by your most concentrated prospects, generally specialized business or consumer publications, remain the most influential. But a hit in *Time* or on *Good Morning, America* can reach a wider potential audience while dramatically reinforcing your company's messages to existing prospects.

Top-down public relations involves the same steps as any other public relations program. Its success lies in its approach and in specifics.

The first step is to evaluate the announcement's importance. The second is choosing the hook. The third is picking

ing the target media. And the fourth is the pitch. Let's look at each one of these issues in more depth.

Some news is simply more important than others to the media. IBM buys Rolm. IBM sells Rolm. Next shows its computer. Lotus finally ships the new version of 1-2-3.

These important announcements don't really demand superb public relations implementation. They'll be covered.

Compaq releases new co-op marketing plan. Hitachi introduces a faster version of a memory.

These announcements are of interest mainly to a very small group. The publications that reach that group will publish them.

The biggest issue is announcements that fall between these two, ones neither of great interest in themselves, nor of interest only to a dedicated audience. For them, the critical question is, "Who cares?" If the answer is, "No one," it's time to think hard or move on to another subject.

One of the true tests of creativity is finding significance for news that's not of obvious importance. One of the best ways to do this, I've found through experience, is the brainstorm. It's especially useful to have participants with varied experiences, and, ideally, some with little knowledge of the company involved or the product. And an informal setting may help.

Some people are simply more creative than others, of course. But true creativity is as often the application of old ideas to new circumstances as it is coming up with completely new ideas. That, after all, is a rare occurrence at best.

With some effort, it's often possible to find angles that can make even a commonplace idea interesting. In some cases, it involves expanding an announcement or augmenting it with additional news.

One obvious scheme is to stage an event or hold an

interesting function. This can work well, but beware of crying "Wolf!" The press isn't that gullible. Burn them once and YOU may get the scars.

Most events are better suited for customers, resellers and employees than the press, but some are truly newsworthy. Even some corny ideas work.

Some of the other standbys to increase interest are celebrities (but make them relevant!), results of polls or surveys, partners and customers. Some attention-getting promotions are highly successful, some best forgotten. The best are worthy of adding attention in their own right, not just ways to make the reporter open the package. Good or bad, however, some reporters hate them, some love them. As a rule newsmagazine and daily newspaper reporters don't wish to receive promotions. At any rate, keep them inexpensive to avoid offending these reporters.

A recent example of two releases we did illustrate the need to find a good hook if you want general attention.

One of our clients, Gazelle Microcircuits, makes high performance programmable logic devices using gallium arsenide substrates instead of silicon. Do you care? If you're a design engineer, or a writer for an engineering magazine, you probably do.

What about a chip that makes a workstation 25 percent faster? That might be of interest, particularly if you spend a lot of time waiting for your computer to finish recalculating a spreadsheet, redraw a complex diagram, or reformat a document from Times Roman to Helvetica.

This example illustrates the differences that caused us to write two releases, one for the dedicated technical press, and one for the general and business press. One got a cover and two cover lines plus articles in all relevant technical magazines. The other got most of a column in the *Wall Street Journal* and coverage on television.

Could one release serve both? Probably not. The technical

detail vital to the engineering publication would create a candidate for one of those clever columns in the daily press about bad engineering writing; the simplification of the other approach might bore the technical expert.

Now to the question of media. This is a sticky one, for I personally enjoy reading *Electronic Engineering Times* and *PC Magazine*. But there's no question that television, daily newspapers and newsmagazines rank higher in some hierarchy of perceptions.

Just for the sake of argument, I'd suggest that hierarchy starts with network TV, then *Time* and *Newsweek,* the big three business magazines and two big dailies *(Business Week, Fortune* and *Forbes; New York Times* and the *Wall Street Journal* and the local daily. They all require a lot of thinking to penetrate in most cases — unless you're blessed with charmed circumstances such as a big company or a real breakthrough.

Besides these big names, there are obviously hundreds of significant publications and broadcasters that you might approach. Dont' forget all the home-town media. They're great for recruiting, employee relations — and stroking the egos of executives who are quoted or pictured.

It's important not to alienate your core contacts at trade publications in the process, however. Don't give so much attention to the general media that you forget who your real friends are — the ones that you deal with often, the ones that report your less-dramatic news and the ones who reach your customers.

Once you've decided on which media to approach, you have to decide how to pitch them. In general, the business and consumer media are less affected by on-going relationships than the trade media, and more impressed with great ideas.

Two secrets to pitching unfamiliar media (or even your best friend): Read the publication and find where and how your story would fit (or watch the program). Then develop that elevator pitch — the one you can deliver in a typical elevator ride. And not the elevator in the World Trade Center, either.

You may not always convince Dan Rather, but chances are you'll do a better job of convincing even a trade book if you take this approach. And you'll probably get more ink (or air time) as well.

March 1989

Arrange Speaking Engagements

One of the most effective ways for a company to assert its leadership — especially in technology — is for its executives to speak at conferences, seminars and forums. And there are plenty of opportunities for them to speak. Almost any meeting of more than a few industry executives has a guest speaker, maybe a number of them. But it's not always obvious how to get on the program. Sometimes it takes a lot of work; sometimes it's impossible. Let's look at the opportunities that are available and how to take advantage of them.

The major categories of talks are:

• Industry conferences like COMDEX or Siggraph,

• Technical conferences such as the International Solid State Circuits Conference,

• Financial conferences such as those sponsored by the American Electronics Association, investment bankers and Technologic Partners,

• Seminars organized by vendors or resellers,

• Conferences arranged by market research firms such as Dataquest, Jim Porter and Ray Freeman or In-Stat, and

• Dinner and lunch meetings of professional groups.

Getting on the program at each requires different approaches. In the first place, many of the positions are by invitation only. Esther Dyson and Stewart Alsop, for example, choose speakers they believe will be interesting and a good draw. It's not easy to convince them to choose someone else. More to the point, they choose speakers based on their personal relationships with the potential speakers. If your president wants to speak at the PC Forum or Agenda 90, he better be president of a very interesting or important company. And he better try to develop a personal relationship with the organizers. Give him their phone numbers and tell him to call.

Likewise, many speakers are chosen for their technical achievements. It would be unseemly to try to convince the organizers of some of the groups to choose you, your client or your company expert to speak.

Similarly, other groups expect you to qualify by presenting a serious paper that is judged by peers or more than peers. The ISSCC and conferences on artificial intelligence, object-oriented languages and other sophisticated esoterica are among these meetings.

Investment bankers sponsor some very interesting and well attended conferences, but they're primarily for their customers or potential customers and for good draws. That shouldn't be a surprise, but I'm constantly amazed at the number of privately held companies that forget the business these firms are in — selling services.

Market researchers typically invite customers and important industry figures (who draw others and could become customers if they aren't already) to speak.

Some important conferences are those sponsored by the American Electronics Association. Their meetings, particularly the annual private and public company gatherings in Monterey, have been vital forums for high-technology companies looking for financing, visibility or better valuation. It's also easy to get an invitation to attend. You pay for your appearance, a straightforward and honest approach. (They do have standards, however.)

Likewise, distributors and other vendors often invite

those from industry to speak at the many seminars they sponsor. Not surprisingly, the speakers they choose are usually their principals.

None of this means that you can't create opportunities. But now we're getting to the heart of the matter, those conferences where hard work and planning can create a chance to talk before a significant audience. These conferences are primarily those important industry meetings like COMDEX, MacWorld, Siggraph, the Design Automation Conference, Autofact, UNIXExpo, etc. They also include professional groups, which are almost always looking for speakers.

In simple terms, the way to speak at these conferences is to organize a good session — and do it first, a long time before the conference. A rule of thumb is to approach the organizers at least a year in advance with your ideas.

The organizer gets to choose the subject. He can choose the speakers — including those from his company, his customers, his partners or even his competitors. He can arrange publicity in advance or invite reporters to the session or hold his own press conference or issue a synopsis after the session.

In short, the only good bet to speak is to arrange it. Otherwise you're at the mercy of others, and those others may well be competitors. I wouldn't want to be the expert from Novell trying to penetrate a panel on LAN software arranged by someone from 3Com, who would likely choose speakers from 3Com, Microsoft and 3Com customers and resellers.

The actual procedure for arranging a panel differs for each conference, but it typically involves proposing a session with a topic and proposed speakers. This session may be approved by the conference organizer, but is more likely referred to a panel of industry experts who judge its worthiness.

Assuming the topic and panelists pass muster, you're in. Of course, you and the speakers have to submit abstracts, slides and even papers. But that can occur a long time after the planning, and close to show time.

Incidentally, I've found it best for the communication with the conference program chairman to come from (or appear to come from) the actual session organizer or moderator, not a public relations specialist or agency. This is especially true for the most prestigious conferences, which act as if industry-leading executives and engineers have nothing better to do than discuss learned topics in a quasi-academic environment.

In summary, it's very easy to get on some panels: You pay for them or provide compelling commercial reasons to the organizer. It's equally difficult to get on other programs. But it's straightforward to speak on others: You plan in advance, have a good and appropriate subject — and good panelists.

However you do it, speaking at industry conferences is a great way to increase the credibility of your firm — and the speaker. It should be a high priority for those striving to be industry leaders, either personally or corporately.

January 1989

Publicize Dull Products

I recently had my ears boxed when I joked about attempts to get press attention for resistors, which I described as "the ultimate in dull products." This comment reflected my days as an editor. Then it was hard to get excited about resistors when Intel was announcing its newest microprocessor or Hewlett-Packard its newest computer.

As you might imagine, the "boxer" works at a respected resistor maker. But his point was well taken. Much written about promotion concentrates on hot new products. It rarely discusses ways to promote unexciting products, perhaps ones made by static companies?

I personally find it satisfying to get good publicity for products most people consider boring. After all, it's not a great trick to get huge amounts of publicity for a NeXT or Apple. Doing a good job for a less exciting product helps turn work into a challenging game. My attitude is, "If you don't look forward to going to work every day, do something else."

What is a dull product? This obviously depends on the perspective of the viewer. I've found the more a reporter relates to a product, the more interesting it is to him. Almost everyone likes consumer products and personal computers. On the other hand, few reporters relate well to electronic components and production equipment. Above all, I've found, almost nobody is interested in mainframe software, no matter how important it is or what it can do for a company.

Fortunately, there's a simple secret for getting attention for less-exciting products: Do a great job. In other words, you have to do everything right and not let any opportunities slip by. Having a compulsive personality can help if you're in this situation.

Of course, sometimes you can make a dull product interesting. That's one of the creative challenges in public relations. One of our clients made paper and related products for computer printers and plotters. You'd think, "What reporter would ever be interested in this stuff when they could be writing about the printers, software and computers involved?" But all they heard about every day was computers, software and printers, so high-tech paper was a nice change.

And if you think about it, computer paper *is* interesting. You know that if you've ever tried to produce sophisticated type and graphics transparencies and hard copy on laser printers, monochrome ink jet printers, color ink jet printers and plotters, all with different demands.

Realistically, you can't make everything interesting. Whether or not you can, you still need to do the same things. Most public relations tactics can work for less-exciting products, but some tactics seem more important.

As always, having good relationships with the right reporters helps a great deal. If they respect you, they're more likely to think of you and call, giving you a better chance to pitch your story. This is a lot more important than if you're a big exciting player, who will get covered anyway.

Beyond knowing the right reporters, it's vital to search published editorial schedules and submit information to the magazines in plenty of time. As we all know, I hope, these published schedules are primarily designed to help the magazine's advertising sales force attract ads, but that doesn't mean they aren't important. Knowing the subject in advance, you might even be able to get into a sidebar, often a better placement than the body of the piece. Most editorial copy in publications is *not* in these surveys, of course, but you don't want to miss being in any relevant ones. You can propose additional subjects, but it's hard to succeed unless the subject is timely or interesting.

The next opportunity is for product introductions. Again, make them superb. Plan in advance. Place technical articles if possible. Provide excellent artwork. Good photographs double the likelihood of acceptance and also double the space for far more than four times the impact.

It's worth pointing out that some products won't receive much coverage in the top books in the field. Fortunately, there are usually other opportunities — in second (or third!) tier magazines, highly specialized publications and related but out-of-field media. These books may even be better since they're not generally as big and packed with competing messages. Some reach your target audience better than the leading magazines in a market. Some also generate more or better leads for the same reasons.

Photos and other artwork provide additional opportunities. Most magazines have photo files, where they search when illustrating survey articles and other stories. Sending good photos and captions in 35 mm color slides and 4 x 5 or larger black and white prints often result in nice hits, sometimes even covers. For this, it's good to have some artistically composed shots and some standard product shots with and without people (realistic shots, not models in designer gowns or business suits bonding ICs).

If you can persuade your engineers and technicians to write articles, they provide great publicity. Both application articles that provide information on how to use a product and tutorial articles that are more general and educational are useful.

Specialized vertical magazines often like clear but simplified tutorial articles. You can sometimes place the same piece in many different magazines in different markets by rewriting the title, lead and examples to fit the industry.

Another good opportunity is customer case histories, which highlight your products. Again, don't expect to place them in the *Wall Street Journal*; most major publications just want customer names and telephone numbers if anything, not pre-written articles.

Many of the best opportunities for direct and possibly printed visibility result from speaking at seminars, trade shows and industry conferences. Sometimes a company that isn't considered an exciting leader can gain attention by organizing and moderating a panel featuring its customers and even competitors.

Leadership in industry associations is another way for a company to gain visibility.

Finally, creative and appropriate promotions can help a company seem more interesting and exciting. As I discussed in my column last month, however, meeting your objectives with promotions isn't always easy.

This list of tactics includes many appropriate for all products. I'd like to throw in two warnings, though.

It may be tempting to try to get attention by associating your company with an exciting one, but I've found that the press is rarely interested. If NeXT is offering your software, it may be worth one phrase in a sentence, but rarely more. Basically, you can get lost if your partners and alliances are *too* newsworthy.

And finally, don't be tempted to exaggerate the importance of your announcements to get press if you ever want to deal with the same reporters again. Most editors have long memories, vast acquaintances, strong opinions and fast presses. You don't want to make them angry with you.

June 1989

Arrange a Great Promotion

One of the standbys of public relations is the "gimmick" promotion aimed at the press and other audiences. Some of these promotions are triumphs, others disasters. In general, they're tricky. You have to be careful to avoid offending people, being ridiculed or spending a lot of money and getting little return.

The biggest goofs I know of arose from lack of common sense, but other problems have resulted from confusion about the aims of the promotions or understanding of the audiences they address.

The first thing to remember is that most promotional ideas — like splashy events — are best aimed at audiences other than the press. They are excellent for dealers and major customers, for example. Don't make the media and analysts the focus, since the press has mixed feelings about the promotions they get.

In particular, don't send promotions to daily papers. Most major newspapers have rules against accepting these items, and receiving them is a nuisance to the reporters.

If you insist on sending promotional material to dailies, make sure that it isn't valuable. At most papers, $5 is the limit.

The trade press is a different matter. Its job is covering the industry, and knowing these things is part of the job. Again, though, the items sent should not cross the boundary to being valuable, for it might seem an attempted bribe to some editors and reporters. (Admittedly, there are some reporters who will take anything you give them, but they're rarely important.)

Beyond that, the promotions should be relevant, classy and non-offensive.

Don't send something just to get attention. It should make a worthwhile point. This point could involve a success for the company, a new product, a teaser for upcoming news or an attempt to get the recipient to a press conference or meeting.

One of the most effective promotions ever was the famous asparagus campaign Advanced Micro Devices mounted ten years ago on its tenth anniversary. It was a campaign that extended far beyond a single item, but was carried through in advertising, collateral, speeches and meetings.

The theme was simple and elegant. When you plant asparagus, it takes years of waiting and careful nurturing of the plants until they start producing. But then they produce the most desirable and elegant of vegetables.

AMD's point was simple. It was like an asparagus bed. After years of development (and supplying second-source ICs), it was now successful and ready to take its place among the major semiconductor producers. The idea apparently came from Jerry Sanders, the company's founder.

As the kickoff of the campagin, AMD sent small wooden crates containing a few stalks of fresh asparagus to key members of the press, making the company's point and getting a lot of attention. I was then editor of *Electronic Business*, and remember well people rushing around the building trying to collect enough asparagus for dinner — it was out of season in New England.

One of our successful promotions a few years ago was to highlight Hewlett-Packard's rising share of computer products sold through dealer channels. We discovered that a major market research firm had been publishing a report that gave HP a significant share of the retail channel.

To make the point, we sent pies to the press (not to other analysts, of course!) with a short release and pie chart about HP's slide of the retail market, quoting the research.

The first thing we learned is that you can't send fruit across state lines — bugs, you know, though I don't know how they'd live in the sugar, much less through the cooking. Most pies can't be shipped, but we found some tasty good pecan-walnut pies that could be.

The promotion succeeded beyond our hopes. In addition to articles about HP's increasing share of the market, there were many references in other articles to HP's greater "piece of the pie." A few reporters even mentioned the promotion itself.

More significantly, reporters began to recognize that HP was a major player in the dealer market.

In general, food seems to be a pretty good promotion, as are classy art posters, T-shirts, sports bags, etc. A lot of editors like to get useful items: Little tool kits, pens and note pads are popular. Most editors have enough paperweights.

Here are some other successful promotions:

• "Clatter controllers" (ear muff) to emphasize the quiet operation of Hewlett-Packard LaserJet printers.

• "Red hots" (cinnamon candy) and jars sent when Software Publishing Corp. shipped its first millionth program.

• Champagne glasses with an invitation to an open house. We knew that few reporters would attend — they rarely do in Silicon Valley — these glasses made the point about the growth and success of the firms.

Not all promotions work. Some offend people. Though

I'm a wine drinker, I don't recommend sending alcohol unless you're sure that the recipient would like to get it. It's complicated to send alcohol across state lines anyway.

Food is usually a good promotion, but the two worst promotions I know of both involved food.

One company sent frozen steaks to reporters. Unfortunately, the steaks defrosted in the process, so reporters ended up with disgusting bloody slabs of meat on their desks, in many cases before they even had their morning coffee. Needless to say, I don't remember the point of the promotion.

Another company sent live lobsters. They were supposed to arrive just before the July 4 vacation. But most didn't. Instead, the editors and reporters came back from a four-day vacation to find thoroughly dead lobsters in their in-baskets. And nothing smells worse than a lobster dead three days.

I have to credit Terry Quinn, an old-time journalist and public relations director for a final example, one aimed at potential customers, not the press. It was successful — though with a twist.

In Belgium, pigeon racing is very popular, and as a promotion, one company decided to exploit this interest. It sent baskets containing homing pigeons to key prospects with a message to fill out a tiny questionnaire, then place it in the small carrier tube on the pigeon's leg and throw the bird out the window.

Belgium is a small country, and the company arranged for salesmen to arrive at the potential customers' sites very quickly, in some cases within 15 minutes or so.

All the pigeons came back but one. Everyone assumed a hawk got it - or maybe a boy with a BB gun. The next week, however, the firm received the tiny questionnaire pasted on a letter that arrived in the mail. "I have recently committed my budget for computers for this year, so don't need to receive information from you. But thank you for the pigeon. It was delicious." *May 1989*

PUBLIC RELATIONS AGENCIES

Hire a Public Relations Agency?

As the founder and president of a public relations agency, I'm often challenged to explain why a corporation should hire an agency instead of simply adding to its own staff. It certainly seems at first glance that added staff would be better. They are likely to know the company's products and operations better. And it sounds cheaper to hire a dedicated person at $40,000 per year than it does to hire part of a person at an agency.

Nevertheless, it often makes sense to hire an agency, whether you have an internal public relations staff or not. It's unlikely that there would be so many agencies around, many of them with numerous savvy clients, unless the agencies had significant value.

Since we have to address this question often, I've tried for years to come up with a credible, concise and comprehensive answer. Fortunately, I don't have to try anymore. One of our clients, a major computer company, answered the question for me. I'm indebted to it for the following comments.

This company is a well-organized firm that requires written plans for all of its people and projects. In our public relations plan, they included a statement of why they hired us. They also specify that 75 percent of the time we work for them will be consulting and planning, only 25 percent implementing programs. This is typical for large companies that have their owm public relations staffs, but new companies without internal public relations experts typically require proportionately more execution.

The company specifies six reasons it uses an agency. I'll add two more at the end of this column.

Objectivity. An agency should be dedicated to your firm and its goals, but shouldn't be a large yes-man. One of the biggest strengths of a good agency is that it has a lot of experience with the press and other clients and knows what works and what doesn't. In particular, it's important for your agency to help set realistic expectations about potential results without beimg considered negative.

A good agency should be able to tell you when a new product deserves major treatment, and when this effort would be wasted. The agency should know when to take a low profile and when to crow. And it should know whether your claims are credible or would be discounted by the press.

It's perfectly reasonable to press the agency for superb results, but not to expect them to do what they know won't work. A good example is the big event. Events, except for major announcements by very newsworthy firms like NeXT, Apple or IBM, should be primarily for dealers, customers, partners, vendors and employees, not the press. If a product is announced properly (unless it's a blockbuster), the press has little need to come to an event. Few reporters need another free meal or another glass of champagne. Yet when we point this out to clients, they never listen. They say, "Steve Jobs got 2000 people to the introduction of the NeXT computer," ignoring the newsworthiness of the person, the company, the computer, the market or even the fact that most of those people weren't reporters.

We've even advertised for account people who can say "no" to clients. It takes confidence for an account representative to do this, one reason we like our staff to have lengthy experience. And this is one of the strengths of a good agency.

Creativity. An agency has to be creative if it's going to help you stand out in a crowded marketplace. Part of this creativity can emulate from those few clever people who always have great ideas, but creativity is often the result of varied experiences and brainstorming by different people in the agency including some who don't work on your account. The best ideas often begin, "When ABC had a problem like that, it did such and such."

Creativity takes many forms. Sometimes it shows itself as wild, attention-getting ideas. Just as often, it's the appropriate application of a familiar idea or process to a specific problem.

Supplemental resources. In many cases, a company needs to apply additional brainpower to its problems. A good agency should be able to provide this additional intelligence in the people who normally work on an account. It should also have additional staff members who have special talents such as technical or market knowledge, writing skills, or financial, community, political or employee relations experience.

Incremental resources. One client calls this "peak horsepower," a phrase only an engineer could love. But the concept is clear. Sometimes your firm needs a lot of extra bodies or minds to get a project done in a short time. This overflow work is a poor reason to hire an agency if that's the major need, and it makes it difficult for the agency to plan its own business so that it can provide the help needed. Nevertheless, clients *do* put on media tours and press conferences, and make major announcements, with insufficient warning and inadequate preparation. An agency can be a big help in getting a company through this heart-stopping process with minimum bruises.

Greater established relationships. Most company public relations staffers naturally concentrate on knowing those influencers most important to the firm. But companies often need to talk to a wider variety of media, perhaps to enter new market segments, new geographic areas or completely new markets. They may need to occasionally talk to political reporters or broadcast media not normally critical to them.

Any agency worth its salt, on the other hand, has a wide range of relationships with many editors, analysts and consultants that serve a variety of markets and readers. And agencies should be able to approach completely new media easily, explaining in terms its reporters can understand, why their client or its products might be interesting to the journalist's readers.

Variety of experience. An agency as a whole generally has a wide range of experiences dealing with varied conditions and circumstances. Sometimes, though widely removed from the apparent needs of a client, these experiences are relevant. We recently compiled a list of the different types of clients our staff had worked on, for example, and discovered experiences very useful to some existing and potential clients.

As an agency, most of our work has been im business-to-business marketing and financial communications for high-technology firms, yet staff members have extensive experience in consumer, health care and sports marketing, plus community and employee relations and public affairs, in some cases having dealt successfully with very demanding situations. Any of these experiences might be appropriate for one of our clients as they grow.

The preceding six items are those our client gave for hiring us and continuing to utilize our services. I might add two more reasons that firm didn't mention, credibility and cost.

Credibility. Experienced public relations counselors should bring a lot of experience and credibility to their advice to management. Internal public relations managers who recognize this can utilize this credibility to help convince their executives to commit to important programs. Experienced outside consultants should have more credibility than staff members, for no matter how experienced the staff member, or how high he or she reports inside a company, the independent counselor probably spends a lot more time talking to other executives if he is doing his job right, and can speak with greater authority.

Cost. It may be surprising, but in many cases, a company saves money by using the right outside agency, perhaps in combination with internal resources. An agency needs direction, but that may best come from management. Supervising an agency may not be a full time job, though an agency needs someone inside a company who can supply answers and make things happen.

We find that at smaller companies, an agency directed by the company president and vice president of marketing is often most cost effective. As companies grow, they should add internal capability, perhaps starting with a strong marketing communications expert who can manage public relations, advertising, collateral, trade show and other agencies. At some point, it may make sense to add internal communications managers who can specialize in functions, products and tactics, using the agency more as consultants on communications issues and to initiate and manage certain critical programs.

Finally, if you take a true comparison of the costs, including overhead, support, wasted time, vacations and so forth, an agency can be very cost effective. I've been through the mathematics many times. And, of course, it's easier to cut back on an agency if conditions warrant, a flexibility not always available with employees.

December 1988

How Big Should an Agency Be?

 $\mathbf{E}$ xecutives of public relations agencies can debate end-lessly about how big an agency should be, but their clients are more likely to wonder how they can get great service and results. In truth, size itself isn't the issue.

There's little question that a larger agency can offer more capability and greater resources than a small agency, but that isn't always what the client needs.

Let's look at why agencies grow, then consider the consequences of that growth. Finally, I'd like to share my optimum solution, one learned through hard experience. It also reflects a bit of crow eating.

Growth occurs for many reasons, including demand from present and prospective clients. Agencies typically attempt to grow in order to generate greater income, to better serve existing clients or attract new clients. Sometimes, however, the reason for the growth is the egos of owners or professional managers.

None of this is bad. The conventional wisdom is that a business that isn't growing isn't well, like Woody Allen's view of relationships in *Annie Hall*. It's also important for many people to say that they run the biggest company in their business, or are growing fastest.

I know. In 1983, my company was the fastest growing public relations agency in the country, according to *O'Dwyer's* listing. We grew 129% and got considerable pub-licity and attention.

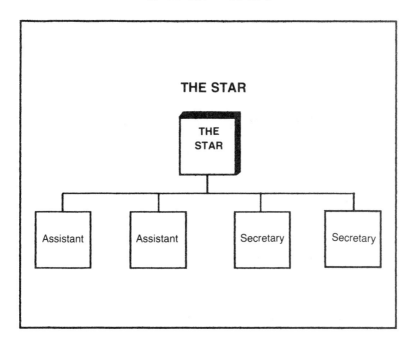

Sadly, this growth was disruptive to clients and staff. We've controlled growth since then, and we and our clients are happier. I'm personally convinced that it's hard to grow rapidly and maintain quality in a service business.

Of course, a larger size implies larger revenues, higher profits, and greater compensation for owners and executives. That can be true, but it isn't automatic. Simple mathematics says that you have to finance growth, and that can only come from profits at most companies.

Alternately, growth from additional services your clients need can be highly desirable. We have added additional reaearch, writing, and international capability (partly by association with other firms or individuals), and significantly beefed up our financial relations strength over the years. All of these steps have benefitted clients who have used them. They're also helped attract clients.

Most of all, however, we have upgraded our staff, hiring more experienced people with better qualifications. Perhaps even more important, we're keeping our senior people longer and making them, not recent graduates, the key client contacts. This has helped our clients more than any other change we have made.

We've also expanded with new offices, a management distraction that rarely benefits existing clients. And we dabbled in collateral, again causing more problems and adding little value — especially not profits!

That doesn't mean that it's not possible to expand effectively, especially if you can find the right people, but that's another headache, an even larger one in some cases.

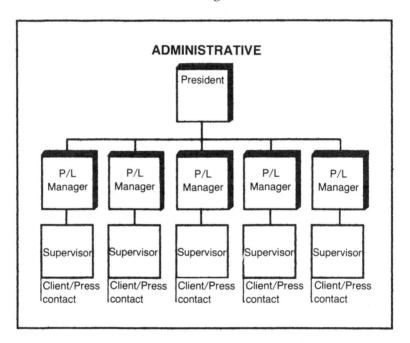

In general, it's better to find excellent partners to offer services that aren't strategic to your firm and concentrate on what you do best. In our case, that's business-to-business strategic and tactical public relations for technology-based companies and related organizations such as financial services, associations and development agencies.

We have about 40 employees and revenue of around $3.5

million. That makes us small compared with Hill & Knowlton or Burson-Marsteller, but we are one of the larger independent players in our market segment.

We believe that we are large enough to offer our clients the services they need, typically strategy and general tactics when they're small, and a greater focus on strategy and other consulting programs as they grow. And I believe that we can continue to serve our clients well if we grow properly.

How does this compare with other agencies? In my view, there are three types of organizations for public relations agencies:

- The star system.
- The administrative company.
- The consultative organization.

The star system is the typical small company with one key expert who tries to be the prime client and press contact and hires others mostly to help him deliver services. This type of agency can't grow to a large size, but it can do a superb job if it recognizes its limits and stays within them.

The organization typical of most large agencies is the administrative one, with layers of supervisors primarily concerned with managing people, revenue and profits. In this type of organization, the client work tends to fall primarily to the lower levels and junior people. The more experienced public relations experts are mostly concerned with organization, politics, new business and profits.

That doesn't mean that these agencies are attempting to maintain the flavor of smaller agencies. Shandwick and Saatchi & Saatchi/Rowland, which have been aggressively buying independent agencies, have stated goals of leaving their acquisition fairly autonomous.

That's great for the former owners, who are now managers, and the clients, but other agencies that have tried similar strategies have been frustrated with some of the entrepreneurs they've acquired.

Finally, there's the consultative approach to organizing a public relations firm. It's similar to a management consulting group, law office or accounting firm. It consists of a number of senior consultants advising clients and driving accounts, with junior personnel implementing specific programs under their direction.

Needless to say, clients love this. They get seasoned experts with extensive experience advising them, plus lower-cost staff to help with projects.

The junior people hate it, of course. They all want to manage accounts, usually before they're ready. That means that clients can't be dependent on them, at least in a high-mobility area like Silicon Valley.

And even though senior counselors have wide experience, they can also call on others in the agency for additional advice or assistance, including the managing consultants, their peers, and other agency resources.

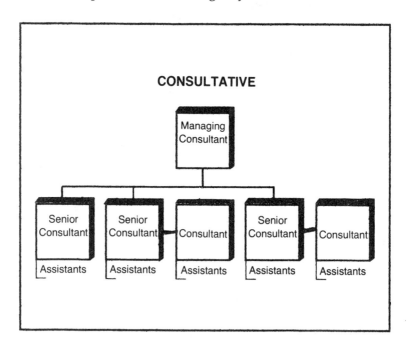

The way this type of organization grows is by amoeba-like growth and division, hopefully within the same company. And this organization can grow to a large size — if management understands what it's trying to do: create a company that serves clients with senior personnel, not simply grow and promote your best public relations people out of public relations functions.

So that's my suggestion of a way to make agency size irrelevant. And that crow I mentioned? In April 1985, *Inc.* magazine ran an article on personal service businesses discussing roughly these same types of organizations. In it, I said I wanted to create a big pyramidal organization.

I learned. I didn't like the isolation, but more significantly, clients didn't either. They felt that they weren't getting the service they wanted and deserved.

So we changed. I suspect some of the other small firms that are growing fast will come to the same conclusion and adopt the same approach over time.

PR WEEK August 1988

Use A Public Relations
Agency Without Commitment

As the president of a reasonably well-known public relations agency, I'm often asked by companies — especially new firms — if we'll take them as clients even though they don't have much money to spend or don't want to spend much.

My answer is generally "no." It's not that I'm cruel and heartless, trying to keep them from getting rich and successful. But I do run a business, and I have many hungry mouths to feed. And we're not interested in working with companies that won't succeed because of insufficient resources or lack of commitment to marketing.

Nevertheless, I'd like to be helpful. That's one of the reasons I write this column, try to speak on public relations and marketing, and participate in certain professional groups.

After thinking about it, though, I'd like to offer some suggestions about the ways companies can take advantage of the knowledge stored within competent public relations agencies without signing up as a full client (which in our case generally requires a minimum commitment of $75,000 or more annually).

Some of these suggestions may not be practical to all, but I know of cases in which all have worked and helped the firms involved.

Read articles and books written by experts. Unfortunately, there's a shortage of good practical books on public relations for technology-based companies. There aren't even very many good books on product-oriented public relations of any type, since traditional public relations professionals have considered community, corporate, employee, and government relations higher callings.

There are some good books on marketing in general, and on high technology in particular. I'd certainly recommend Trout and Ries' *Positioning: The Battle for Your Mind*, McKenna's *The Regis Touch*, and Davidow's *Marketing High Technology* as three must-reads, though none say much about public relations per se.

Many publications specialize in marketing and public relations, including *Marketing Computers*, and they contain much useful tutorial information about public relations. Some newsletters are excellent for tactical details. I especially recommend *High Technology PR News* and the *Bulldog Reporter*. Aside from other useful content, these publications sometimes include hints from public relations experts.

Attend seminars, professional meetings, and classes featuring experts. Local and national professional organizations have many meetings, and sometimes they have excellent programs. Many college courses on public relations subjects, especially night courses, are taught by experienced professionals, and they can be very helpful and practical. Most standard college public relations programs, by contrast, are rather theoretical and impractical.

A growing number of for-profit organizations are holding short courses in public relations, and they tend to feature noted and competent speakers.

Pretend you're a serious new business prospect ready to spend a lot. You'd be amazed how much information and advice you can get without paying. Don't assume that it's worthless because it's free. Listen carefully and consider the advice seriously.

Hire a public relations firm's experts for a few hours of consultation. Some agencies won't do this, but others will, particularly if you appeal to the egos of the principals or hold out the hope for future business.

One note: Make sure that you really get an expert for this advice, but it doesn't have to be the person with his name on the door. At our agency, for example, many people know more than I do about many things and even have to tell me what to say before I go into meetings with clients.

If you do decide to hire an expert for a few hours, don't ask for a written report. That's where the price really escalates. Just talk and listen and take notes. Even better, bring along a compulsive underling to take notes and prepare a summary. You'll save a bundle and probably get excellent advice.

Get the expert involved in your firm. Give or sell him some stock at a low price. It doesn't have to be a huge amount to get attention.

Put the expert on your board. Chances are that you can benefit from his marketing expertise, industry knowledge and contacts.

Try to trade at least part of the fees for stock in your firm, or for something else of value if you make a useful business machine or attractive consumer product. (P.S. Our lawyer tells us not to do this. He recommends the previous tactic of putting a person on your board instead. Some of my competitors may not have the same lawyer, however.)

Get the firm to handle only part of your account. You may most need initial consultation to help you identify your best opportunities or decide on your company introduction strategy, for example. You may need help in planning a program to help determine and communicate your position. You may need someone to execute a specific program, such as writing technical articles or reaching a wide variety of editorial contacts. Many agencies will take on these partial tasks.

Don't forget that there are many knowledgeable individuals who aren't well known but could be of great help. These include asocial people who choose to work alone rather than in agencies, other professionals and retired experts. Some talented people who have full-time jobs at corporations have time to moonlight, since many corporate jobs are less demanding than those at most agencies and they don't encounter as great a potential for conflict of interest.

Likewise, some small agencies might be ideal for your needs if you don't need wide contacts or varied experiences, or as many resources. And finally, don't forget that I know these tricks. Try them on my competitors, not on me.

May 1988

Maintain Good Agency-Client Relations

The relationships between a public relations agency and its client should be a rewarding partnership, but it often turns into a constant battle. As head of an agency, I've learned a lot, mostly through some unpleasant experiences.

I'd like to suggest some ways to avoid these pitfalls. Some of these suggestions may seem odd — and I suppose they could come back to haunt me. Nevertheless, I've seen so many problems in relations between agencies and clients that I believe that this is an important subject to discuss.

Poor communication. Poor communication is really the heart of most client-agency problems. It's certainly ironic that people in the communications business sometimes have so much trouble managing their own communications.

Some of this may be due to poor personal habits or training, lack of attention, poor presentation skills or misunderstanding of the communications process.

I'm convinced that lack of empathy is often the base cause of communications problems. Some people are obviously more empathetic than others. But if you're in a communications role, you have to learn to put yourself in another person's place. It is definitely a skill that can be acquired, perhaps by taking workshops or attending seminars.

Distrust. Distrust — even paranoia — is a common problem between agencies and their internal public relations contacts. Many internal public relations people find external agencies and their staffs intimidating and threatening.

Part of the reason for this distrust may be that external agency personnel are often more experienced, better connected and more aggressive. And if they're doing their job right, they should have greater access to and credibility at high levels of the corporation.

Unwillingness to bring up problems. Most people are uncomfortable talking about things that will displease other people. Instead, they let the problems fester until they reach a point where it is difficult to recover. For that reason, I think it's vital to set up ways to force people to bring up problems. I'll discuss some ways later in this column.

Incompetence or inexperience. One problem that can afflict both agencies and corporations is incompetent people. It's unpleasant to consider, but it's a common situation. Far too many people end up in jobs for which they are unprepared, either by lack of training or lack of aptitude.

The only way to deal with an incompetent person is to recognize the situation and go over the person's head. It's never a pleasant situation. I find it best for equals to talk; it's generally inappropriate for an account executive to tell a company president that the internal public relations person is incompetent. It's better for a supervisor or agency principal to get involved.

Simple inexperience is somewhat easier to deal with than stupidity. But every company has a right to expect sufficient experience and judgment from its agency. If the working level contact doesn't have it, the client should demand someone with more experience.

That doesn't necessarily mean that you have to deal only with the agency head. Many clients seem to have illusions about working with the agency head, but I can say from my own experience with clients, the press and vendors that you rarely get the best results from trying to get the boss involved in details (except in a very small organization). Better to use him or her for big purposes and leave the real work to experienced staff and management.

Unrealistic expectations. A final contributing problem is unrealistic expectations. It's hard to convince some clients that they simply can't expect to be on the cover of *Time*, featured in *Business Week*, or even the subject of a lead story in *The Wall Street Journal*. Their egos are too big.

One client who fired us honestly believed that the announcement of his mainframe software product was as important as the continuing problems of the Bank of America, and couldn't understand why the local business writer for *The New York Times* was too busy to see him.

How do you deal with these problems? Part of the solution is better training of those involved, and much of the burden obviously has to fall on the agency. After all, the client is the customer. But there are specific ways to avoid some of the biggest hurdles.

First, you need to establish a number of different relationships in an agency-client partnership. Account executives often work closely with public relations managers. But there's also a need for supervisors to talk to marketing management, and for agency principals to work with corporate executives.

Corny as it may seem, I believe that trying to get to know the people you work with by getting together for lunch or dinner can go a long way toward reducing or heading off many possible conflicts.

Nevertheless, with all the priorities of both companies and agencies, it is hard to consistently maintain all these contacts. One of the best ways to do this is to force regularly scheduled reviews with all levels present. That gives everyone involved a chance to monitor the progress of the program, make necessary corrections, and perhaps most important, provide a forum to bring up problems in a positive environment.

A regular review also encourages everyone to pay attention to priorities. Even if we're no longer in school, that regular report card is still an important motivator.

January 1987

Combine Public Relations With Advertising?

Executives of corporations often wonder whether Public Relations should be part of marketing or whether it better fits in somewhere else. In a similar vein, does it make sense to have separate advertising and public relations agencies or combine them in one "Marketing communications" agency?

I regard myself as relatively unbiased on the first question, very opinionated on the second. I'd like to present the contrasting arguments for both issues, then give you my recommendations.

Public relations functions fit into corporations in many different ways. Some of these relationships seem rational, matching the importance of public relations to the company, while other arrangements may more reflect management's attitude toward the public relations staff itself.

The worst case is for marketing communications and public relations to report to some unrelated function headed by someone with little interest in it. Examples are customer support, technical publications, product marketing or sales.

One approach that sounds good is to assign all communications, both marketing and investor-oriented, to a director of communications, perhaps even a vice president of communications (the CCO or chief communications officer?). This appeals to the marketing communications professional, since it suggests the company holds both the head of communications and the function in high stead.

In practice, companies with this arrangement often seem more interested in their stock price than in their customers, a warning sign about the firm's long-term prospects. In practice, this may mean that marketing-oriented communications functions don't get much attention or credibility within executive ranks.

A fairly common arrangement at customer-oriented companies is for the corporate communications function to report through the marketing chain, perhaps to the vice president or director of marketing. In practice, this head communications person is usually an advertising person, a consequence of the attitude of many executives that people who handle big budgets (advertising) must be more senior than those with smaller budgets (public relations).

In spite of this, this is usually an excellent arrangement if the head of public relations is an assertive person with excellent access to and relations with a president who values the function.

Investor relations often reports directly to the chief financial officer, a good arrangement if IR talks to PR, and everyone remembers that the business press is as important in talking to customers as it is in talking to investors.

As is often true in staff positions, the personalities of individual communications people including those in public relations can have more impact on their ability to do their jobs than their titles and reporting relationships. And so do the priorities of top management.

No matter where marketing public relations fits in an organization, it's imperative that its activities be coordinated with other communications functions within and outside a company. In particular, this includes advertising, sales promotion, investor relations, and, as appropriate, employee, community and government relations. It's a rare company where this happens, either because of territoriality or oversight, but it can have a big impact on the quality of the communications process.

One continuing discussion in industrial and business marketing is whether it's better to have an agency that combines marketing communications functions, or whether it's better to have separate agencies. After all, it's clearly important to coordinate efforts, ensuring that advertising, public relations and other marketing communications have similar objectives and messages and don't contradict and cancel each other's efforts.

The greatest argument for a combined agency is this common management, but it also promises reduced duplication of effort.

In practice, however, the needs and skills of the advertising and public relations are so different that there is rarely real benefit in combining the two.

Public relations is primarily an educational tool, and depends for its success on the credibility of the practitioners and processes to the gatekeepers who determine what is published or ignored.

Advertising is far more a sales tool, depending more on obvious persuasion and the ability to choose and pay for media.

Even the way agencies charge affects the process. Advertising agencies generally receive much of their revenue from commissions, so management tends to make decisions and focus on this process. That leaves the public relations staff second-class citizens.

Most members of the press don't want to deal with ad agencies. They regard them as sales people who don't understand the editorial process and don't value its independence. And if this is true even for most trade editors, imagine the feeling of daily newspaper journalists, who are suspicious enough even of public relations people!

The major, consumer-oriented agencies learned this long ago. Though most have public relations arms, they keep them independent, and in practice, they really do operate independently in most cases — except occasionally in sales calls.

Because of this dichotomy, most public relations professionals prefer to work at public relations agencies or in corporations where they enjoy more respect. And few first-rate advertising professionals would choose to work at a public relations agency that just does a little advertising to support public relations programs such as tombstones, ego-driven corporate advertising and advertorials.

If this discussion seems to show a bias, it's not because my firm is a PR-only agency, but that I've chosen to have a PR-only agency. I think it's best for us and for our clients, and many of my colleagues who run the better advertising and PR agencies have shed the activities that don't fit into the mainstream of their expertise and are concentrating on their specialties.

February 1989